# POSITIVE QUOTATIONS & TIPS

## (English Edition)



## VIJAYKUMAR GUMMADI

NOTION PRESS

**NOTION PRESS**

**India. Singapore. Malaysia.**

Published by Notion Press 2022




ISBN 979-888805770-4

Dedicated

to

my daughter

Gummadi Pavani

# Foreword

This Book is a beautiful compilation of  life and work affirming Positive Quotes & Tips that are useful to you throughout your life at all times. These expressions are derived from world's greatest thinking minds.

This Book covers nine areas of Life and Work i.e.  1)Love; 2)Feminism;  3)Money;  4)Happiness;  5)Human  Nature; 6)Anxiety  &  Depression;  7)Good  Diet  &  Obesity; 8)Governance & Politics And  9)Life & Work  Planning.

More than 1000 versatile as well as unique Quotes & Tips were presented in this book.

This Book Guides you and shows you correct direction like a North-Star.

This Book gives sound practical advice with applied Some Quotes & Tips are Inspiring & Motivating, some are funny and some make's you to re-think creatively.

This book removes all your confusion and guides you like wisdom.

This book "POSITIVE QUOTATIONS & TIPS" is a beautiful motivational and inspirational reference book for your home as well as for your office.

# Positive Quotations & Tips

## <u>Contents</u>

# 1.LOVE

Love is human existence. Without love humans as well as society can't survive.

Human race progressed ancient to modern society only by human to human bonding of love.

Human history is full of examples of personalities who have achieved wonders with love in different spheres of life and society.

Wonder of the world and UNESCO world heritage site Tajmahal was constructed for 22 years by Mugal Emperor Shah Jahan for passion and love of his wife Mumtaz that mega monument mesmerises everyone even today.

Love is the essence and glory of all individual achievements whether it is their profession or personal life.

♣♠♣

# 1.0 Love

## Contents

♣♣♣*(1.1)*♣♣♣
# FRAGRANCE OF LOVE
♣♣♣*(1.1.1)*♣♣♣

Love consists exhibition of articulated expressions and elegant physical expressions.

♣♣♣*(1.1.2)*♣♣♣

Love makes you do wonderful things when you are intimate.

♣♣♣*(1.1.3)*♣♣♣

Expression of love is too beautiful in infinite ways.

♣♣♣*(1.1.4)*♣♣♣

Love creates aura with undeniable sweet aroma with your magnetic personality.

♣♣♣*(1.1.5)*♣♣♣

Everybody yields to sweet fragrance of love there is exception.

♣♣♣*(1.2)*♣♣♣
# EMPATHY OF LOVE
♣♣♣*(1.2.1)*♣♣♣

Love gives empathy to understand misunderstanding of loved ones.

♣♣♣*(1.2.2)*♣♣♣

Love forgives loved. Love never intentionally hurts any one. You need not be sorry in love.

♣♣♣*(1.3)*♣♣♣
# SECRETS IN LOVE
♣♣♣*(1.3.1)*♣♣♣

Love has no secrets, love hides nothing.

♣♣♣*(1.3.2)*♣♣♣

Love tells only truth and never lies.

♣♣♣*(1.3.3)*♣♣♣

True Love is infallible.

♣♣♣*(1.4)*♣♣♣
# CRITICISIM IN LOVE

*♣♣♣(1.4.1)♣♣♣*

When you Love much,  you criticize much,  because you care much.

*♣♣♣(1.4.2)♣♣♣*

True love guides and corrects.

*♣♣♣(1.4.3)♣♣♣*

Who loved only knows the power of love.


*♣♣♣(1.5)♣♣♣*

## CHANGE IN LOVE

*♣♣♣(1.5.1)♣♣♣*

Absence of love is a trigger and initiator for change.

*♣♣♣(1.5.2)♣♣♣*

Betrayed Love makes beast.

*♣♣♣(1.5.3)♣♣♣*

Love changes with time and circumstances.


*♣♣♣(1.6)♣♣♣*

## LOVE BONDING

*♣♣♣(1.6.1)♣♣♣*

Love generates ceaseless infinite ripples of  desire.

*♣♣♣(1.6.2)♣♣♣*

Love is very strong mutual bonding, it is merciless, )♣♣♣
Love makes people to work for mutual good.

*♣♣♣(1.6.4)♣♣♣*

Loves wishes good for beloved.

*♣♣♣(1.6.5)♣♣♣*

It can't tolerate others in between.

*♣♣♣(1.6.3*

Love is felt only by those who love.

*♣♣♣(1.6.6)♣♣♣*

Lovers will have single thought.

*♣♣♣(1.6.7)♣♣♣*

Loved one's can't be spontaneously detachable.

*♣♣♣(1.6.8)♣♣♣*

If you love a thing means you wanted it to be well and good.

### ♣♠♣(1.7)♣♠♣
## LIFE AND LOVE
### ♣♠♣(1.7.1)♣♠♣
Self love and selfless love is the reason to be alive.
### ♣♠♣(1.7.2)♣♠♣
You don't feel life is as if living without love.
### ♣♠♣(1.7.3)♣♠♣
Love is absolute stillness where time stops for others time passes by.

### ♣♠♣(1.8)♣♠♣
## CRAVING OF LOVE
### ♣♠♣(1.8.1)♣♠♣
Love gives feeling of self fulfilment and self satisfaction and ignorance of others.
### ♣♠♣(1.8.2)♣♠♣
Love can't wait, it demands immediate attention.
### ♣♠♣(1.8.3)♣♠♣
Love is a alignment if not treated by giving passion it makes them mad.

### ♣♠♣(1.9)♣♠♣
## SUFFERING OF LOVE
### ♣♠♣(1.9.1)♣♠♣
More the love more are the sufferings.
### ♣♠♣(1.9.2)♣♠♣
You will feel pain of suffering without love.
### ♣♠♣(1.9.3)♣♠♣
Love is the cure for anguish.
### ♣♠♣(1.9.4)♣♠♣
Love gives courage to enjoy pleasure as well as pain to suffer.

### ♣♠♣(1.10)♣♠♣

# BLIND LOVE

*♣♣♣(1.10.1)♣♣♣*

When you are in love you can't see your surroundings.

*♣♣♣(1.10.2)♣♣♣*

When love is detached, you are attached to your surrounding world.

*♣♣♣(1.10.3)♣♣♣*

When you are in love you are not the part of universe.

*♣♣♣(1.10.4)♣♣♣*

Love alters your perception about others, other than your beloved.

*♣♣♣(1.10.5)♣♣♣*

Love is a displayer of amplified admiration.

*♣♣♣(1.10.6)♣♣♣*

Love makes  you see things in differently.


*♣♣♣(1.11)♣♣♣*

# VULNERABILITY OF LOVE

*♣♣♣(1.11.1)♣♣♣*

Love make you vulnerable and compulsive against your intuition.

*♣♣♣(1.11.2)♣♣♣*

Love makes your conscience biased.

*♣♣♣(1.11.3)♣♣♣*

True Love is forever, it's never a opportunity.

*♣♣♣(1.11.4)♣♣♣*

Due to compulsive behaviour love sometimes resembles disability of mind.

*♣♣♣(1.11.5)♣♣♣*

Our love shows our vulnerability.

*♣♣♣(1.11.6)♣♣♣*

Wise can become fools in love.

*♣♣♣(1.11.7)♣♣♣*

You can't conquer those you love.

*♣♣♣(1.11.8)♣♣♣*

Love is taken for granted.

### ♣♣♣*(1.12)*♣♣♣
## SENSE OF LOVE
### ♣♣♣*(1.12.1)*♣♣♣
Love supersedes all other senses including hunger.
### ♣♣♣*(1.12.2)*♣♣♣
Hunger of love is more craving than hunger.

### ♣♣♣*(1.13)*♣♣♣
## SELF LOVE
### ♣♣♣*(1.13.1)*♣♣♣
Love is proven only by loving.
### ♣♣♣*(1.13.2)*♣♣♣
When others don't love us we don't love our self.

### ♣♣♣*(1.14)*♣♣♣
## TRANSFORMATION IN LOVE
### ♣♣♣*(1.14.1)*♣♣♣
Love illuminates, transforms and enables to live in harmony.
### ♣♣♣*(1.14.2)*♣♣♣
Love knows only to honour love.
### ♣♣♣*(1.14.3)*♣♣♣
Love makes you human.

### ♣♣♣*(1.15)*♣♣♣
## LOVE IN MODERN LIFESTYLE
### ♣♣♣*(1.15.1)*♣♣♣
Love  cease to exist in modern Lifestyle.

### ♣♣♣*(1.16)*♣♣♣
## NEUROSIS IN LOVE
### ♣♣♣*(1.16.1)*♣♣♣
Where there is no room for love in heart there is only hate.

♣♣♣*(1.16.2)*♣♣♣
You never hate those you love.
♣♣♣*(1.16.3)*♣♣♣
Without love it is neurosis.

♣♣♣*(1.17)*♣♣♣
## VIRTUAL LOVE
♣♣♣*(1.17.1)*♣♣♣
Love is only mental bond.
♣♣♣*(1.17.2)*♣♣♣
Love makes you earthy by bonding.
♣♣♣*(1.17.3)*♣♣♣
Time is a test for love.

♣♣♣*(1.18)*♣♣♣
## SELFLESS LOVE
♣♣♣*(1.18.1)*♣♣♣
Love is gifting of self to others.
♣♣♣*(1.18.2)*♣♣♣
It is difficult to be judicious while in love.
♣♣♣*(1.18.3)*♣♣♣
Love and politics simultaneously don't occur.

♣♣♣*(1.19)*♣♣♣
## WOUNDS OF LOVE
♣♣♣*(1.19.1)*♣♣♣
)True love attack heart and mind simultaneously.
♣♣♣*(1.19.2)*♣♣♣
You are deeply wounded by those whomever you deeply love.
♣♣♣*(1.19.3)*♣♣♣
Love injury lasts life long.
♣♣♣*(1.19.4)*♣♣♣
Wound of loss of love is deepest that can't be ever healed.

♣♣♣*(1.20)*♣♣♣

# EXISTENCE AND LOVE

♣♣♣(1.20.1)♣♣♣

Love keeps you alive.

♣♣♣(1.20.2)♣♣♣

Love is our existence.

♣♣♣(1.20.3)♣♣♣

Love is psychic energy that fuels mind.

♣♣♣(1.20.4)♣♣♣

Love converts hell into heaven.

♣♣♣(1.21)♣♣♣

# HEART OF LOVE

♣♣♣(1.21.1)♣♣♣

You only love with your heart because it got only one eye where as you don't love your mind because it got too many eyes.

♣♣♣(1.22)♣♣♣

# CONDITIONS OF LOVE

♣♣♣(1.22.1)♣♣♣

When you Love someone it is unconditional, sometimes it proves to be too expensive.

♣♣♣(1.22.2)♣♣♣

True love doesn't owe anything  from anyone.

♣♣♣(1.23)♣♣♣

# ATTENTION TO LOVE

♣♣♣(1.23.1)♣♣♣

1Just loving not enough but you must also leave enough room for your love to sustain and  flourish.

♣♣♣(1.24)♣♣♣

# SURPRISE OF LOVE

♣♣♣(1.24.1)♣♣♣

Miraculous things do happen because people choose love over life.

*♣♣♣(1.24.2)♣♣♣*

Love surprises.

*♣♣♣(1.24.3)♣♣♣*

Burden of love is heavier than any other thing.

*♣♣♣(1.25)♣♣♣*

## THIRST OF LOVE

*♣♣♣(1.25.1)♣♣♣*

Love creates a never ending thirst.

*♣♣♣(1.25.2)♣♣♣*

Love is never receding spring.

*♣♣♣(1.26)♣♣♣*

## RISK IN LOVE

*♣♣♣(1.26.1)♣♣♣*

Love feels no risk of risk and no impossibility.

*♣♣♣(1.26.2)♣♣♣*

Love is blind persistence.

*♣♣♣(1.26.3)♣♣♣*

Love gives capacity to endure.

*♣♣♣(1.26.4)♣♣♣*

True love will have unaltering same passion to all circumstances.

*♣♣♣(1.27)♣♣♣*

## WOMEN IN LOVE

*♣♣♣(1.27.1)♣♣♣*

Women known only loving.

*♣♣♣(1.27.2)♣♣♣*

Where there is no love there will be no women.

*♣♣♣(1.28)♣♣♣*

## REFERENCES

♣♣♣*(1.28.1)*♣♣♣
Collected  works  of  KAHLIL GIBRAN
♣♣♣

# 2.FEMINISM

There is distinct difference between men and women. Men are earthy where as women are blend of divine and earthy as they are capable of creating new life.

Girls and Women are integral bond and glue to society as well as families. This is a undeniable fact.

Women possess unique characteristics that are essential for sustainable world. Unfortunately Women are discriminated whether they are in developed or developing countries. The discrimination may be actual or psychological. They are never treated equal for what they deserve.

# 2.Feminism

## Contents

## ♣♣♣(2.1)♣♣♣
# ACHIEVEMENT
### ♣♣♣(2.1.1)♣♣♣
Nourishing and cherishing women are behind every great man.
### ♣♣♣(2.1.2)♣♣♣
Women are shaped by their fate.

## ♣♣♣(2.2)♣♣♣
# BEHAVIOUR
### ♣♣♣(2.2.1)♣♣♣
All women's behaviour in general subjected to man.
### ♣♣♣(2.2.2)♣♣♣
It's society norm for women for compulsive behaviour under social pressure.

## ♣♣♣(2.3)♣♣♣
# BOREDOM
### ♣♣♣(2.3.1)♣♣♣
When women are happy they don't bore you with history.

## ♣♣♣(2.4)♣♣♣
# CHANGE IN SOCIETY
### ♣♣♣(2.4.1)♣♣♣
Unhappy women are root cause for triggering change.
### ♣♣♣(2.4.2)♣♣♣
Women's influence on society is deep and everlasting.
### ♣♣♣(2.4.3)♣♣♣
If you want to change society change women's attitude.

## ♣♣♣(2.5)♣♣♣
# CONDUCIVE ATMOSPHERE
### ♣♣♣(2.5.1)♣♣♣
Only smiling women makes thriving world.
### ♣♣♣(2.5.2)♣♣♣
Women create a magical atmosphere.

♣♣♣*(2.5.3)*♣♣♣
Women kill boredom and make lively atmosphere.

♣♣♣*(2.6)*♣♣♣
# CONTROL
♣♣♣*(2.6.1)*♣♣♣
Women who live by men have no control over their lives.

♣♣♣*(2.7)*♣♣♣
# CREATION
♣♣♣*(2.7.1)*♣♣♣
Women create complete world.
♣♣♣*(2.7.2)*♣♣♣
Women can't destroy by default.

♣♣♣*(2.8)*♣♣♣
# CULTURE
♣♣♣*(2.8.1)*♣♣♣
Culture is a reflection of collective personality of all women.

♣♣♣*(2.9)*♣♣♣
# DISCRIMINATION
♣♣♣*(2.9.1)*♣♣♣
here is clandestine discrimination of women in men's attitude.

♣♣♣*(2.10)*♣♣♣
# EMOTIONS
♣♣♣*(2.10.1)*♣♣♣
Women's emotions can run extreme on either side than men.

♣♣♣*(2.11)*♣♣♣
# EMPOWERMENT
♣♣♣*(2.11.1)*♣♣♣

Women's empowerment will be reality only when there is change in men's attitude to women and women's attitude to themselves.

*♣♣♣(2.11.2)♣♣♣*

Women's unity and solidarity are important for their liberation.

*♣♣♣(2.12)♣♣♣*
## EQUALITY

*♣♣♣(2.12.1)♣♣♣*

Once we grant equal rights to women, they will lead men due to their inherent superior talents.

*♣♣♣(2.12.2)♣♣♣*

For keeping supremacy and to control women they are intentionally kept inferior.

*♣♣♣(2.12.3)♣♣♣*

Free choice and allowing them to do what they want is equality for women.

*♣♣♣(2.13)♣♣♣*
## FEELINGS & AFFECTIONS

*♣♣♣(2.13.1)♣♣♣*

Men's history is full of feelings whereas women's history is full of affections.

*♣♣♣(2.14)♣♣♣*
## FLEXIBILITY

*♣♣♣(2.14.1)♣♣♣*

Flexibility and adaptability to circumstances is inherent to women.

*♣♣♣(2.15)♣♣♣*
## FOCUS

*♣♣♣(2.15.2)♣♣♣*

Women have excellent persistent focus of sticking to task at hand.

### ♣♣♣*(2.16)*♣♣♣
# GOODNESS
### ♣♣♣*(2.16.1)*♣♣♣
No one looks for good women.
### ♣♣♣*(2.16.2)*♣♣♣
Goodness of women spreads good essence.

### ♣♣♣*(2.17)*♣♣♣
# HANDLING UNCERTAINITIES
### ♣♣♣*(2.17.1)*♣♣♣
Educated women are better at handling uncertainties.

### ♣♣♣*(2.18)*♣♣♣
# HEART AND MIND
### ♣♣♣*(2.18.1)*♣♣♣
Women's heart seeks not mind, where as men's mind seeks not heart.

### ♣♣♣*(2.19)*♣♣♣
# IDENTITY
### ♣♣♣*(2.19.1)*♣♣♣
In most parts of the world women identity is defined by their existing culture and their men.

### ♣♣♣*(2.20)*♣♣♣
# INFERIORITY COMPLEX
### ♣♣♣*(2.20.1)*♣♣♣
Women though they are deserving and capable when compared to men due to inferiority complex and lack of ambition they are held back.
### ♣♣♣*(2.20.2)*♣♣♣
Society inherently treats women inferior.
### ♣♣♣*(2.20.3)*♣♣♣
It's feeling of being women that causes inferiority.

♣♣♣ *(2.21)* ♣♣♣
# INTERESTING AGE
♣♣♣ *(2.21.1)* ♣♣♣
Women are more fascinating between thirty five to forty.


♣♣♣ *(2.22)* ♣♣♣
# ISSUES
♣♣♣ *(2.22.1)* ♣♣♣
Issues that affect women are central issues that affect all.
♣♣♣ *(2.22.2)* ♣♣♣
Women's issues are automatically given priority.


♣♣♣ *(2.23)* ♣♣♣
# JUSTICE AND AFFECTION
♣♣♣ *(2.23.1)* ♣♣♣
Women give importance to affection more than justice.


♣♣♣ *(2.24)* ♣♣♣
# LOYALTY
♣♣♣ *(2.24.1)* ♣♣♣
Women remains loyal forever to those whom she has given her heart.


♣♣♣ *(2.25)* ♣♣♣
# MATERIALISM
♣♣♣ *(2.25.1)* ♣♣♣
2.26.1)Materialism doesn't exist without women.
♣♣♣ *(2.25.2)* ♣♣♣
2.26.2)Money got gravity due to women.


♣♣♣ *(2.26)* ♣♣♣
# MENS LONGING
♣♣♣ *(2.26.1)* ♣♣♣

Men's unconscious fear and longing for feminism is inherently embedded in their genes. It's a natural reflux.

♣♣♣*(2.27)*♣♣♣
## MEN's VULNERABILITY
♣♣♣*(2.27.1)*♣♣♣
Man is not open to man but to women.

♣♣♣*(2.28)*♣♣♣
## MINDSET
♣♣♣*(2.28.1)*♣♣♣
Mindset of people and women's rights are inseparable.

♣♣♣*(2.29)*♣♣♣
## MODERN THINKING
♣♣♣*(2.29.1)*♣♣♣
Women's are stuck in primitive thinking and rarely have modern thinking.

♣♣♣*(2.30)*♣♣♣
## MOTIVATION
♣♣♣*(2.30.1)*♣♣♣
Women encourage and create ambition for achievement, success and power in others.

♣♣♣*(2.31)*♣♣♣
## NATURE
♣♣♣*(2.31.1)*♣♣♣
Women's nature is natural law of nature.
♣♣♣*(2.31.2)*♣♣♣
Nature of women is similar to water.
♣♣♣*(2.31.3)*♣♣♣
By nature women are better than men.
♣♣♣*(2.31.4)*♣♣♣
Women know perfect ways to treat with softness and kindness.

♣♣♣*(2.31.5)*♣♣♣
Women are inbuilt human.

♣♣♣*(2.31.6)*♣♣♣
Default nature of women is calm and passive.

♣♣♣*(2.32)*♣♣♣
## ORGANISING

♣♣♣*(2.32.1)*♣♣♣
Women are very good at organising.

♣♣♣*(2.32.2)*♣♣♣
You must include women for systematic organising.

♣♣♣*(2.33)*♣♣♣
## PERSONALITY

♣♣♣*(2.33.1)*♣♣♣
Original personality of women is known directly but not through their men.

♣♣♣*(2.34)*♣♣♣
## POLITICS

♣♣♣*(2.34.1)*♣♣♣
Women never stop when she speaks of politics.

♣♣♣*(2.35)*♣♣♣
## PESSIMISTIC NATURE

♣♣♣*(2.35.1)*♣♣♣
Cursing women are pessimistic women by nature.

♣♣♣*(2.36)*♣♣♣
## PROTECTION

♣♣♣*(2.36.1)*♣♣♣
Women shouldn't depend upon others for protection.

♣♣♣*(2.37)*♣♣♣
## RELATIONSHIPS

♣♣♣(2.37.1)♣♣♣

Women give more care and emphasis on relationships than men.

♣♣♣(2.38)♣♣♣

# RIGHT ATTITUDE

♣♣♣(2.38.1)♣♣♣

By default women trys to be right.

♣♣♣(2.39)♣♣♣

# SACRIFISE

♣♣♣(2.39.1)♣♣♣

Women undermines their ambitions for fulfilling others wishes.

♣♣♣(2.39.2)♣♣♣

Women are limited only by men.

♣♣♣(2.39.3)♣♣♣

Women are conditioned not to upset men.

♣♣♣(2.39.4)♣♣♣

Women are expected to renounce normal life for others.

♣♣♣(2.40)♣♣♣

# SOCIAL PROGRESS

♣♣♣(2.40.1)♣♣♣

Honour to rights of women is a reflection of true social progress.

♣♣♣(2.40.2)♣♣♣

Respect for women's rights is foundation to social progress.

♣♣♣(2.41)♣♣♣

# SOLUTIONS

♣♣♣(2.41.1)♣♣♣

Women has her own ways to do things.

♣♣♣(2.42)♣♣♣

# SUPPORT

♣♣♣*(2.42.1)*♣♣♣

People with good will only support women's moral resistance.

♣♣♣*(2.43)*♣♣♣

## TEACHING SKILLS

♣♣♣*(2.43.1)*♣♣♣

No one can teach better than women.

♣♣♣*(2.44)*♣♣♣

## TEAM

♣♣♣*(2.44.1)*♣♣♣

Women are better part of teams.

♣♣♣*(2.45)*♣♣♣

## UNDERSTANDING

♣♣♣*(2.45.1)*♣♣♣

Understanding a women is a unsolvable puzzle.

♣♣♣*(2.45.2)*♣♣♣

It is not possible to predict what women thinks.

♣♣♣*(2.45.3)*♣♣♣

When you love you need not understand a woman.

♣♣♣*(2.45.4)*♣♣♣

Women understand more though they have less awareness.

♣♣♣*(2.46)*♣♣♣

## UNITY IN DIVERSITY

♣♣♣*(2.46.1)*♣♣♣

Women are the reason to bring and keep human race close together despite differences and diversity.

♣♣♣*(2.47)*♣♣♣

## UPLIFTMENT

♣♣♣*(2.47.1)*♣♣♣

Men rarely put efforts to uplift women  from domestic  level to social level.

♣♣♣(2.48)♣♣♣
# VIRTUAL AGE
♣♣♣(2.48.1)♣♣♣
You will feel women's age by her love not by physical age.

♣♣♣(2.49)♣♣♣
# VULNERABILITY
♣♣♣(2.49.1)♣♣♣
Women are vulnerable as they are poor at defending both physically and mentally.

♣♣♣(2.50)♣♣♣
# WELFARE
♣♣♣(2.50.1)♣♣♣
Real welfare means wellbeing of women.

♣♣♣(2.51)♣♣♣
# WOMEN AND WOMEN
♣♣♣(2.51.1)♣♣♣
Women and Women are natural friends.

♣♣♣(2.52)♣♣♣
# WORK AND HOME
♣♣♣(2.52.1)♣♣♣
Probably there may not be any culture who doesn't discriminate women's equality at home and work.

♣♣♣

# 3.MONEY

Money is root cause of almost all personal, social and society problems. Money definitely helps in reducing human suffering in the world.

Whole society revolves directly or indirectly around money. Money attracts many and many things automatically.

Doing well with money is basic and fundamental requirement in this modern chaotic and  dynamic world.

Most people under illusion feels managing money and investing decisions require knowledge of mathematics and calculations and experience.

For managing money first we must know about money.

♣♠♣

# 3.Money

## Contents

## ♣♣♣*(3.1)*♣♣♣
# ABILITIES
### ♣♣♣*(3.1.1)*♣♣♣
Lack of money can limit some personality qualities and attributes. Lacking money is never a obstacle for your achievement, however Lack of creative idea is

### ♣♣♣*(3.1.2)*♣♣♣
Every human has his worth. When money is absent you need talent to replace

### ♣♣♣*(3.1.3)*♣♣♣
ll direct or indirect human achievements are due to wealth. Richness gives you wings


## ♣♣♣*(3.2)*♣♣♣
# ACCOUNTING
### ♣♣♣*(3.2.1)*♣♣♣
Accounting can be deceptive or diverting hence verify it always. Conspiracy coexists with accounting

### ♣♣♣*(3.2.2)*♣♣♣
Due to synergy effect value of total is never equals to sum of individuals values


## ♣♣♣*(3.3)*♣♣♣
# BEHAVIOR
### ♣♣♣*(3.3.1)*♣♣♣
Just look and observe at those who has money

### ♣♣♣*(3.3.2)*♣♣♣
Same money speaks differently in different pockets

### ♣♣♣*(3.3.3)*♣♣♣
Those who believe money is most powerful will do anything for money

### ♣♣♣*(3.3.4)*♣♣♣
Wealth tends to incline your life towards luxury  and laziness and poverty inclines your life towards bare essential comforts and aggressive

*♣♣♣(3.3.5)♣♣♣*

Everybody cares and does something about money.
Humbleness and prosperity rarely coexist. Humanity is
forgotten when some people are lost in passion of money

*♣♣♣(3.3.6)♣♣♣*

Rich mans acts are always viewed as special. Rich are distinctly
different. It is difficult to be sensitive and rich simultaneously.
Rich are misunderstood easily. Money creates more enemies
than friends

*♣♣♣(3.3.7)♣♣♣*

Earn with mind, spend with heart. Fortune adds to grace. You
will be wonderful if you don't care money. Being rich needn't
be a indicator of smartness

*♣♣♣(3.3.8)♣♣♣*

Money converts dishonest as honest. Money speaks. Money
makes people to listen. All they see is money. Rich are
exempted adhering to woes and promises.

*♣♣♣(3.3.9)♣♣♣*

Where your treasure there your heart. Spending money creates
a feeling of being rich

*♣♣♣(3.3.10)♣♣♣*

Unshared  richness makes poor perspective of you in others


*♣♣♣(3.4)♣♣♣*

# BEING HUMAN

*♣♣♣(3.4.1)♣♣♣*

Whether you are rich or poor but mortal remains  same

*♣♣♣(3.4.2)♣♣♣*

Difference between humans and inhuman is money


*♣♣♣(3.5)♣♣♣*

# BUYING

*♣♣♣(3.5.1)♣♣♣*

Buying is addicted pleasure

*♣♣♣(3.5.2)♣♣♣*

Money alone facilitates exchange. Everything to be brought with money

♣♣♣*(3.5.3)*♣♣♣

Your choice is the way you spend money

♣♣♣*(3.6)*♣♣♣
## CHILDREN
♣♣♣*(3.6.1)*♣♣♣

Children are affected by their parent socioeconomic condition

♣♣♣*(3.7)*♣♣♣
## COMPOUNDING
♣♣♣*(3.7.1)*♣♣♣

3Compounding effect of money is simple if you save little every month you will get little when you are in need

♣♣♣*(3.7.2)*♣♣♣

Best method to compound money is just not to spend. Money compounding is very important parameter for investment

♣♣♣*(3.7.3)*♣♣♣

3Money seeds money. Money encourages to make more money. It is difficult to earn first seed

♣♣♣*(3.8)*♣♣♣
## CONSCIENCE
♣♣♣*(3.8.1)*♣♣♣

Heart by default gives preferential treatment to money but it should be your conscience that must make it last preference

♣♣♣*(3.9)*♣♣♣
## CONTENT
♣♣♣*(3.9.1)*♣♣♣

Life will be easy and comfortable when you live within your means. Contentment is creator of greatest wealth. In general no one is content hence no one is rich

♣♣♣*(3.10)*♣♣♣
## CONTROL
♣♣♣*(3.10.1)*♣♣♣
Limiting money at disposal enables you to spend on what you like and not on what you dislike

♣♣♣*(3.10.2)*♣♣♣
Spending is a incurable disease hence needs to be controlled. Money is misused when it is made handy. Easy money without control encourages easy go

♣♣♣*(3.10.3)*♣♣♣
Money disappears in no time and appears only after prolonged time. Hence control on money is must. If unchecked, humans take things for granted

♣♣♣*(3.10.4)*♣♣♣
Money certainly ruins him who don't know how to manage

♣♣♣*(3.10.5)*♣♣♣
Keeping money is more difficult than earning money


♣♣♣*(3.11)*♣♣♣
## DEBT
♣♣♣*(3.11.1)*♣♣♣
People forget what they owe unless remained. When you cannot pay you would not pay

♣♣♣*(3.11.2)*♣♣♣
You can know value of money by your ability to borrow

♣♣♣*(3.11.3)*♣♣♣
Greed, insecurity and optimism are main reasons for debt


♣♣♣*(3.12)*♣♣♣
## DIFFERENT TREATMENT
♣♣♣*(3.12.1)*♣♣♣
Men and men are different and differently treated only by their extent of financial burden and income


♣♣♣*(3.13)*♣♣♣

# EARNING

### ♣♣♣ *(3.13.1)* ♣♣♣

ou cannot smell money. Wealth is scarce. Time is money. More the effort to gain money more you feel difficult to catch it. Great wealth requires greatest labour

### ♣♣♣ *(3.13.2)* ♣♣♣

Earning money has nothing to do with intelligence but with few good behavioral skills

### ♣♣♣ *(3.13.3)* ♣♣♣

Behaviour is most important for earning and spending money

### ♣♣♣ *(3.13.4)* ♣♣♣

Everyone has their own money models which is crucial for earning. Earning money is imagination of visualizing invisible

### ♣♣♣ *(3.13.5)* ♣♣♣

History doesn't repeat for earning money, remember all tomorrows opportunities are unique, be attentive

### ♣♣♣ *(3.13.6)* ♣♣♣

Ability to stick is important for money earning. Pessimism holds you back for earning money

### ♣♣♣ *(3.13.7)* ♣♣♣

Becoming rich is always a collective effort rarely a individual effort

### ♣♣♣ *(3.13.8)* ♣♣♣

Even those who work for only pleasure also seek money

### ♣♣♣ *(3.13.9)* ♣♣♣

Friendship hardly brings money

### ♣♣♣ *(3.14)* ♣♣♣

# EDUCATION

### ♣♣♣ *(3.14.1)* ♣♣♣

Educations costs money, it is never free

### ♣♣♣ *(3.15)* ♣♣♣

# ENJOYMENT

### ♣♣♣ *(3.15.1)* ♣♣♣

Wealth is to be enjoyed

### ♣♣♣(3.16)♣♣♣
# EVIL
### ♣♣♣(3.16.1)♣♣♣
Directly or indirectly Money is root cause of evil. It induces and instigates to think to do evil for gain of money.
### ♣♣♣(3.16.2)♣♣♣
Money can smooth inconveniences of life by bribing

### ♣♣♣(3.17)♣♣♣
# EXPENDITURE
### ♣♣♣(3.17.1)♣♣♣
For survival you must limit your habits to limitation of your net income

### ♣♣♣(3.18)♣♣♣
# FIGHTING
### ♣♣♣(3.18.1)♣♣♣
Money divides people. Money is root cause for most direct or indirect internal fighting. Longest surviving purse wins war
### ♣♣♣(3.18.2)♣♣♣
All good nature and behaviour ends when it is question of money. Infinite source of money is the root cause of unrest and differences. Money is the reason for all politics
### ♣♣♣(3.18.3)♣♣♣
People rarely quarrel with their bread and butter

### ♣♣♣(3.19)♣♣♣
# FINANCE
### ♣♣♣(3.19.1)♣♣♣
Cascading of money from its appearance upto disappearance is called finance
### ♣♣♣(3.19.2)♣♣♣
Without goals ruins your financial health

♣♣♣*(3.19.3)*♣♣♣
Lack of understanding and being crazy in decision making are
the root causes for many financial crisis
♣♣♣*(3.19.4)*♣♣♣
Having money is only better solution for financial problems

♣♣♣*(3.20)*♣♣♣
## FREE
♣♣♣*(3.20.1)*♣♣♣
There are no such things as free, either you have to pay directly
or indirectly

♣♣♣*(3.21)*♣♣♣
## HAPPINESS
♣♣♣*(3.21.1)*♣♣♣
Happiness has nothing to do either with money or with poverty
♣♣♣*(3.21.2)*♣♣♣
Spiritualism forces you to think people can be happy without
money. It gives psychological tranquillity

♣♣♣*(3.22)*♣♣♣
## HONESTY
♣♣♣*(3.22.1)*♣♣♣
It is almost very difficult to make honest money by complying
all morals and ethics. Always you have to trade-off somewhere
♣♣♣*(3.22.2)*♣♣♣
You cannot become honestly wealthy.  Honesty can never
amass large fortune

♣♣♣*(3.23)*♣♣♣
## INFLUENCE
♣♣♣*(3.23.1)*♣♣♣
Instant money does automatic magic
♣♣♣*(3.23.2)*♣♣♣
People's are different under magnetic field influence of money

*♣♣(3.23.3)♣♣*

Majority of people can be administratively controlled with the influence of money in modern era

*♣♣(3.23.4)♣♣*

Whether you like money or not but the fact is money runs everything in your life

*♣♣(3.23.5)♣♣*

Money is far more persuasive than other things

*♣♣(3.23.6)♣♣*

Money can conquer anything either  directly or indirectly

*♣♣(3.23.7)♣♣*

Wealth liberates you from many things

*♣♣(3.23.8)♣♣*

Money serves as face mask for face ugliness

*♣♣(3.23.9)♣♣*

Money is capable of answering all things

*♣♣(3.23.10)♣♣*

Money surely makes things better. Money can buy time. No money no service. Wealth can confer favors.

*♣♣(3.23.11)♣♣*

Wealthy are by default enjoys upper hand. Money is obedient solder. Wealth gives greatest leverage. Money confuses all

*♣♣(3.23.12)♣♣*

Wealth is a religion. All are firm believers of religion of money


*♣♣(3.24)♣♣*

# INFORMATION

*♣♣(3.24.1)♣♣*

Modern times neither rich nor poor are isolated information is available to all


*♣♣(3.25)♣♣*

# LAW

*♣♣(3.25.1)♣♣*

Respect for law of land depends upon individuals wealth

♣♣♣*(3.25.2)*♣♣♣
It is much easier to do harm than good w.r.t. wealth

♣♣♣*(3.26)*♣♣♣
## LIFE
♣♣♣*(3.26.1)*♣♣♣
Wealth cannot make life. Money is prose of life

♣♣♣*(3.27)*♣♣♣
## LOVE
♣♣♣*(3.27.1)*♣♣♣
Love of money is most dangerous passion of all passions, if
unchecked
♣♣♣*(3.27.2)*♣♣♣
Money is the causation of either war or love
♣♣♣*(3.27.3)*♣♣♣
Frequent counting of accumulated money indicates your thirst
for money
♣♣♣*(3.27.4)*♣♣♣
Passion to become rich is comparative in nature

♣♣♣*(3.28)*♣♣♣
## MORALS
♣♣♣*(3.28.1)*♣♣♣
If you stick to your morals you are bound to lose money
♣♣♣*(3.28.2)*♣♣♣
Money is the main cause for most demoralizing acts and
behaviours
♣♣♣*(3.28.3)*♣♣♣
Money Camouflages and hides many shortfalls, sins and faults.
Money encourages to lie
♣♣♣*(3.28.4)*♣♣♣
When you replace god with money you are replacing good with
evil in your life
♣♣♣*(3.28.5)*♣♣♣

Fair means or unfair means money is treated as money at the end in world

♣♣♣*(3.29)*♣♣♣
## 3.30
# MOTIVATION
♣♣♣*(3.29.1)*♣♣♣
Money is never a motivation for anyone. However real motivation is excitement for gaining money
♣♣♣*(3.29.2)*♣♣♣
Love of money and want of money are two principle motivational factors

♣♣♣*(3.30)*♣♣♣
# OLD AGED
♣♣♣*(3.30.1)*♣♣♣
You can't be old without money. Need of money for aged is a necessary

♣♣♣*(3.31)*♣♣♣
# PESSIMISM
♣♣♣*(3.31.1)*♣♣♣
Lack of money is direct or indirect root cause of all pessimism

♣♣♣*(3.32)*♣♣♣
# POVERTY
♣♣♣*(3.32.1)*♣♣♣
Poverty is spending money even before you have it
♣♣♣*(3.32.2)*♣♣♣
Without money it is incomplete and doesn't make sense. Wealth helps helpless
♣♣♣*(3.32.3)*♣♣♣
Only scarce not abundant think of money. Poor only knows value and goodness of giving

♣♣♣*(3.33)*♣♣♣
# POWER

♣♣♣*(3.34.1)*♣♣♣
Money plus networking unbeatable

♣♣♣*(3.33.2)*♣♣♣
Money has mysterious nexus with power and love. Money has power sense

♣♣♣*(3.34)*♣♣♣
# PRIORITIES

♣♣♣*(3.34.1)*♣♣♣
Priorities of money is individual to individual it can be anything from lifesaving to luxury

♣♣♣*(3.34.2)*♣♣♣
Money habit is most difficult habit to change or remove

♣♣♣*(3.35)*♣♣♣
# REALITY

♣♣♣*(3.35.1)*♣♣♣
When you live in dream you pay for dream hence try to live in reality

♣♣♣*(3.36)*♣♣♣
# RISK

♣♣♣*(3.36.1)*♣♣♣
Financial risk and uncertainties are part of life and are unavoidable.

♣♣♣*(3.36.2)*♣♣♣
Luck and risk are twin siblings, their contribution decides our financial wellbeing

♣♣♣*(3.36.3)*♣♣♣
For earning money you must know when to stop taking risk

♣♣♣*(3.36.4)*♣♣♣
You must avoid speculation  of money either if you have or if you don't have

*(3.36.5)*

Best opportunity to make money is during chaos

*(3.37)*
# SAVING
*(3.37.1)*

Doing what you want not what people want saves money.
Savings are created by spending less

*(3.38)*
# SCIENCE
*(3.38.1)*

Science is useful for ensuring equality of wealth

*(3.39)*
# SOCIETY
*(3.39.1)*

Money fuels motion in the world. Money makes world go
around. All businesses are run by other people's money
*(3.39.2)*

Language of money is a universal language and is understood
by all irrespective their individual native languages
*(3.39.3)*

There are informal complying social protocols for rich
*(3.39.4)*

Money is reason for all universal devotion. Money is most
important thing in the world
*(3.39.5)*

Society is called affluent when there is no difference between
luxuries and necessaries
*(3.39.6)*

Socialism cannot be practiced without money
*(3.39.7)*

Economic faults arise out of inequalities in distribution of
wealth

♣♣♣*(3.40)*♣♣♣
# TRAUMA
♣♣♣*(3.40.1)*♣♣♣
Money is the greatest source of anxiety whether you have it or not
♣♣♣*(3.40.2)*♣♣♣
Trauma of loss of money is more profound than any other wound
♣♣♣*(3.40.3)*♣♣♣
Money is biggest burden of life as felt by humans. More money more problems
♣♣♣*(3.40.4)*♣♣♣
Money dissolves most of the worries

♣♣♣*(3.41)*♣♣♣
# TRUST
♣♣♣*(3.41.1)*♣♣♣
When you spend large amounts of money, trust non and verify everyone
♣♣♣*(3.41.2)*♣♣♣
Spend and invest money on trustable
♣♣♣*(3.41.3)*♣♣♣
Never believe anyone w.r.t. substantial amount of money
♣♣♣*(3.41.4)*♣♣♣
Invest money in what you trust

♣♣♣*(3.42)*♣♣♣
# WEALTH
♣♣♣*(3.42.1)*♣♣♣
You should be sincere to become rich. Sustainable income as well as savings can only keep you wealthy. When you stop spending you will have enough money in life
♣♣♣*(3.42.2)*♣♣♣
Real richness is ability to make use of wealth

♣♣♣*(3.42.3)*♣♣♣
When you cannot count your money you are wealthy

♣♣♣*(3.42.4)*♣♣♣
Naturally riches are bestowed to spiritually good people


♣♣♣*(3.43)*♣♣♣
## WISE

♣♣♣*(3.43.1)*♣♣♣
Difference between wise and unwise is where you hold money,
in heart or in mind

♣♣♣*(3.43.2)*♣♣♣
Wise uses and unwise misuses wealth

♣♣♣*(3.43.3)*♣♣♣
You can feel essence and goodness  of money only when it is
spread

♣♣♣*(3.43.4)*♣♣♣
Life is greatest wealth


♣♣♣*(3.44)*♣♣♣
## WOMEN

♣♣♣*(3.44.1)*♣♣♣
Women must have her own money

♣♣♣*(3.44.2)*♣♣♣
Money gets meaning due to women


♣♣♣*(3.45)*♣♣♣
## WORRIES

♣♣♣*(3.45.1)*♣♣♣
Only those who are financially secured never think of money

♣♣♣

# 4.HAPPINESS

Your attitude and thinking will be good when you are happy. Not only that you will be more ethical, moral, empathetic and productive when happy.

Ròot cause for most of the personal and society  problems is unhappiness.

Modern lifestyle has replaced room of optimism with pessimism.

Negativity is many folds attractive than positivity and it is difficult to escape its  trap either knowingly or unknowingly.

This book shows the ways to get rid off negative thoughts and choose happy life. It cultivates positive attitude and balanced life in this chaotic modern world.

We have presented here  132 nos TIPS for happiness in a very simple way.

Happiness will make you innovative, creative and prepares you to face challenges.

♣♣♣

♣♣♣(4.1)♣♣♣
Ability to admire without any desire is the character of happiest person.

♣♣♣(4.2)♣♣♣
Society feels prosperity is happiness.

♣♣♣(4.3)♣♣♣
True happiness is detachment.

♣♣♣(4.4)♣♣♣
Individually you can be happy only with mind but collectively you can be happy only with heart.

♣♣♣(4.5)♣♣♣
Happiness will flourish and sustain with daily small gains but not with sudden big gains.

♣♣♣(4.6)♣♣♣
Humans experience intense emotional happiness in depth from very little things.

♣♣♣(4.7)♣♣♣
Amplitude of experience happiness is very high where as duration of happiness is finite.

♣♣♣(4.8)♣♣♣
Worst daily trauma of humans is comparing present experiences with past by retrieving historical happy memories.

♣♣♣(4.9)♣♣♣
Human outward quest for happiness is main reason for unhappiness.

♣♣♣(4.10)♣♣♣
Really what brings happiness is unknown to individual.

♣♣♣(4.11)♣♣♣
Happiness is a derivative.

♣♣♣(4.12)♣♣♣
Happiest people are just as they are. They don't need any reason to be happy.

♣♣♣(4.13)♣♣♣
In reality one is never as happy or unhappy as on thinks or feels, its purely imaginary.

♣♣♣*(4.14)*♣♣♣
Without psychological acceptance one can never be happy.
♣♣♣*(4.15)*♣♣♣
Little happiness makes you open.
♣♣♣*(4.16)*♣♣♣
Memories of experience of happiness are everlasting.
♣♣♣*(4.17)*♣♣♣
Happiness is just imagination.
♣♣♣*(4.18)*♣♣♣
Good memory makes you unhappy.
♣♣♣*(4.19)*♣♣♣
Empathetic personalities cannot be happy.
♣♣♣*(4.20)*♣♣♣
Happiness is not a state but journey.
♣♣♣*(4.21)*♣♣♣
Essence of happiness spreads.
♣♣♣*(4.22)*♣♣♣
Shared happiness is exponentially compounded.
♣♣♣*(4.23)*♣♣♣
For your well being others happiness is important not yours.
♣♣♣*(4.24)*♣♣♣
Understanding exists only with happiness.
♣♣♣*(4.25)*♣♣♣
Happiness creates a feeling of fullfillness.
♣♣♣*(4.26)*♣♣♣
Happiness bonds souls by love.
♣♣♣*(4.27)*♣♣♣
By default you wakeup with happiness in morning.
♣♣♣*(4.28)*♣♣♣
Prolonged happiness is unbearable.
♣♣♣*(4.29)*♣♣♣
Happiness is a reflection of health.
♣♣♣*(4.30)*♣♣♣
Tranquil mind is a home for happiness.
♣♣♣*(4.31)*♣♣♣

Happiness is a torch makes your conscience alive.

♣♠♣(4.32)♠♣♠

We alone make our lives years of unhappy.

♣♠♣(4.33)♠♣♠

Comparison and too much expectations makes you feel unhappy.

♣♠♣(4.34)♠♣♠

Control of passions makes your life happy.

♣♠♣(4.35)♠♣♠

Happiness is the state consciousness of reality of your values.

♣♠♣(4.36)♠♣♠

Happiness exists where ever you are nowhere else.

♣♠♣(4.37)♠♣♠

Happiness creates a sensation of feeling good all over.

♣♠♣(4.38)♠♣♠

Happiness is a synchronous equilibrium state of achievement in between 1)thinking, 2)saying and 3)doing.

♣♠♣(4.39)♠♣♠

4Taking risk is part of achievement of happiness  but not avoiding.

♣♠♣(4.40)♠♣♠

Happiness is a permanently engraved memory.

♣♠♣(4.41)♠♣♠

Being loved gives happiness.

♣♠♣(4.42)♠♣♠

Happy heart complements medicine in curing disease.

♣♠♣(4.43)♠♣♠

True wisdom creates sustained  happiness.

♣♠♣(4.44)♠♣♠

Joy is a profound higher state beyond happiness.

♣♠♣(4.45)♠♣♠

Joy is a force behind power.

♣♠♣(4.46)♠♣♠

If you are happy you will illuminate happiness in others.

♣♠♣(4.47)♠♣♠

Happiness is bestowed to be happy and to keep others happy.

***(4.48)***

If you like what you do, you will be happy.

***(4.49)***

Being comfortable with conscience seeds happiness.

***(4.50)***

Your happiness will sustain as long as your attitude towards things and people is optimistic.

***(4.51)***

Non attachment is a foundation to trigger happiness.

***(4.52)***

Fulfilling your desires won't create happiness rather limiting desires.

***(4.53)***

Happy man has a tranquil and peaceful mind.

***(4.54)***

Cheerfulness prolongs life and makes life more pleasurable and mindful.

***(4.55)***

Happiness acts like torch and makes mind to think with conscience.

***(4.56)***

A happy man is a emotionless man.

***(4.57)***

Only secure people can feel happiness.

***(4.58)***

Pause of pain is a pleasure.

***(4.59)***

Your pleasure is extent of your attachment to your senses.

***(4.60)***

People are lack of empathy to understand others pleasures.

***(4.61)***

Pleasure of happiness makes life long engraved impression.

***(4.62)***

People are compelled under the influence of the their favourite pleasures.

♣♣♣(4.63)♣♣♣

Dissent seeds, if happiness is rationalized.

♣♣♣(4.64)♣♣♣

At the end of the day only domestic happiness remains with you.

♣♣♣(4.65)♣♣♣

Humans life's are difficult but same objective to live i.e. happiness.

♣♣♣(4.66)♣♣♣

Happiness is fulfillment of differed craving.

♣♣♣(4.67)♣♣♣

To make people happy just change their external environment not their mindset.

♣♣♣(4.68)♣♣♣

Happiness makes you good.

♣♣♣(4.69)♣♣♣

Indulge in anything that produces joy.

♣♣♣(4.70)♣♣♣

We believe others to be happy than they are and than we are.

♣♣♣(4.71)♣♣♣

We all wish to be happier than rest.

♣♣♣(4.72)♣♣♣

Smile dissolves anger and angst.

♣♣♣(4.73)♣♣♣

Happiness can't be achieved directly.

♣♣♣(4.74)♣♣♣

Your own effort your own happiness.

♣♣♣(4.75)♣♣♣

Happiness makes you moral.

♣♣♣(4.76)♣♣♣

Follow your Joy.

♣♣♣(4.77)♣♣♣

Happiness is a freedom from pain and disturbing mind.

♣♣♣(4.78)♣♣♣
Only if you are happy you can make others happy.
♣♣♣(4.79)♣♣♣
Happiness comes and goes.
♣♣♣(4.80)♣♣♣
To enjoy happiness you must endure pains attached with it first.
♣♣♣(4.81)♣♣♣
Cheerfulness is a tube light of mind.
♣♣♣(4.82)♣♣♣
You can achieve happiness only after eliminating all your emotions.
♣♣♣(4.83)♣♣♣
State of humans depends upon music of pleasures and pains.
♣♣♣(4.84)♣♣♣
You can be happy only if you overcome your selfishness.
♣♣♣(4.85)♣♣♣
Perfect happiness is not common.
♣♣♣(4.86)♣♣♣
Happiness makes you generous.
♣♣♣(4.87)♣♣♣
World doesn't criticize a happy man.
♣♣♣(4.88)♣♣♣
You don't need controls when you are happy.
♣♣♣(4.89)♣♣♣
Man will always crave for more happiness.
♣♣♣(4.90)♣♣♣
Happiness gives strength to our strengths.
♣♣♣(4.91)♣♣♣
You are prevented to be happy because you want to be  more happy.
♣♣♣(4.92)♣♣♣
Accept things that comes your way like water you will never be unhappy.
♣♣♣(4.93)♣♣♣

Visualize yourself just as you are.

♣♣♣(4.94)♣♣♣

Your happiness depends upon  how beautiful you make your inner world.

♣♣♣(4.95)♣♣♣

Every morning feel exited about life.

♣♣♣(4.96)♣♣♣

Be thankful for another precious day.

♣♣♣(4.97)♣♣♣

See wonderful aspects in everyone around you.

♣♣♣(4.98)♣♣♣

Develop ability to see positive side of others.

♣♣♣(4.99)♣♣♣

Express positive aspects of people around you.

♣♣♣(4.100)♣♣♣

You will gain happiness only if you make others happy.

♣♣♣(4.101)♣♣♣

Keep realistic ideals.

♣♣♣(4.102)♣♣♣

clear mental picture of your ideal.

♣♣♣(4.103)♣♣♣

Fear dissolves all hopes and feelings of happiness.

♣♣♣(4.104)♣♣♣

Don't carry emotional baggage of the past and future.

♣♣♣(4.105)♣♣♣

Have relaxed and open conversations.

♣♣♣(4.106)♣♣♣

Feel and create positive self image which will protect you from negativity.

♣♣♣(4.107)♣♣♣

Stop finding faults in others.

♣♣♣(4.108)♣♣♣

You are hurt only due to your attitude.

♣♣♣(4.109)♣♣♣

Never blame others.

♣♣♣(4.110)♣♣♣
Hardwork shields you from criticism.
♣♣♣(4.111)♣♣♣
Express your individuality constructively.
♣♣♣(4.112)♣♣♣
Never encroach others happiness.
♣♣♣(4.113)♣♣♣
Develop enough self assertiveness and self confidence and never seek approval of others.
♣♣♣(4.114)♣♣♣
Perception of reality and understanding of reality both are not same.
♣♣♣(4.115)♣♣♣
Pain resides in inside. Never be trapped by past and look forward.
♣♣♣(4.116)♣♣♣
Create more room in your heart to be flexible enough to accommodate more personalities.
♣♣♣(4.117)♣♣♣
Choose area of interest that you truly love.
♣♣♣(4.118)♣♣♣
Restraint consciously; being animal by default we think negatively.
♣♣♣(4.119)♣♣♣
Replace negative thinking with constructive positive thinking.
♣♣♣(4.120)♣♣♣
You love for others should be unconditional.
♣♣♣(4.121)♣♣♣
Remember our views are limited by our self centered view.
♣♣♣(4.122)♣♣♣
Always keep something to live for.
♣♣♣(4.123)♣♣♣
Distinguish between your happiness and happiness of people around you.
♣♣♣(4.124)♣♣♣

You need to live true to yourself.

♣♣♣*(4.125)*♣♣♣

Understand different types of people.

♣♣♣*(4.126)*♣♣♣

You have to address your personal problems first.

♣♣♣*(4.127)*♣♣♣

Have good relationships and don't keep excessive self ♣♣♣

♣♣♣*(4.128)*♣♣♣

Balance your earnings and expenditures.

♣♣♣*(4.129)*♣♣♣

Self reflection cleans your personality.

♣♣♣*(4.130)*♣♣♣

Remove rust of mind but positive attitude.

♣♣♣*(4.131)*♣♣♣

Realize you only exist in love.

♣♣♣*(4.132)*♣♣♣

Never try to control others.

♣♣♣

# 5.HUMAN NATURE

We have built more walls than bridges across world in between people. More is the advancement more is the human to human isolation. Next generation communication and internet technologies further fuelling to existing human isolation and differences.

The words compassion and empathy are permanently removed from human dictionaries.

Our human lives are disturbed due to inhumanity and chaos is prevailing everywhere.

There is no more room for accommodating for humanness and understanding humans in world.

Here we have presented 149 TIPS about Human Nature.

♣♣♣(5.1)♣♣♣

Root of human nature is same where as modes of expressions are different

♣♣♣(5.2)♣♣♣

Human nature cravings can ever be completely satisfied by anyone

♣♣♣(5.3)♣♣♣

If unchecked, humans take things for granted

♣♣♣(5.4)♣♣♣

When human nature is biased it is impossible to think straight

♣♣♣(5.5)♣♣♣

You can't make think humans with animal instincts

♣♣♣(5.6)♣♣♣

Being human is to optimise perfection by not seeking absolute perfection

♣♣♣(5.7)♣♣♣

Touch of nature makes us feel kids of nature

♣♣♣(5.8)♣♣♣

Good human nature makes feel better than well educated

♣♣♣(5.9)♣♣♣

Well performed human duty should be with duty discharged with judicious human rights

♣♣♣(5.10)♣♣♣

Few are brave enough to maintain human rights

♣♣♣(5.11)♣♣♣

Unless you won't fight you won't get your rights

♣♣♣(5.12)♣♣♣

All humans are born equal

♣♣♣(5.13)♣♣♣

HumanRights are reality only by implementing

♣♣♣(5.14)♣♣♣

For maintaining world order prevention of human oppression is more important than prevention of human sin

♣♣♣(5.15)♣♣♣

When thinking of mind is human you are optimistic and
mentally healthy

♣♣♣(5.16)♣♣♣

Social work enables to address and help in healing of society
disorders

♣♣♣(5.17)♣♣♣

To be good is to sacrifice something

♣♣♣(5.18)♣♣♣

Human honestly and altruism makes people uncomfortable and
unhappy

♣♣♣(5.19)♣♣♣

Being human we can't ignore humanity

♣♣♣(5.20)♣♣♣

Pure humanity is divine

♣♣♣(5.21)♣♣♣

Mankind lost is controlled by evil thinking of mind

♣♣♣(5.22)♣♣♣

Human knowledge so much finite that can't even predict
happening in uncertainty

♣♣♣(5.23)♣♣♣

Man is bestowed with good and great strength that he don't
want

♣♣♣(5.24)♣♣♣

Keeping optimistic attitude of laughter at every situation
prevents you from weeping in life

♣♣♣(5.25)♣♣♣

Significance of man is his significance for universe

♣♣♣(5.26)♣♣♣

Man's world is world of necessity and freedom

♣♣♣(5.27)♣♣♣

Man's nature is limited by his necessity

♣♣♣(5.28)♣♣♣

Man's senses can ever fulfil satisfaction

♣♣♣(5.29)♣♣♣

Human nature changes with time

♣♣♣ *(5.30)* ♣♣♣

For pleasure of life you should not repeat your moments

♣♣♣ *(5.31)* ♣♣♣

Humans are self annihilating in modern era with so called modern

♣♣♣ *(5.32)* ♣♣♣

In this age you find only bad and worse people

♣♣♣ *(5.33)* ♣♣♣

Humans when unused can become sick

♣♣♣ *(5.34)* ♣♣♣

Humans isolate themselves with individualism from surroundings

♣♣♣ *(5.35)* ♣♣♣

Speculation of risk is alone unique to humans

♣♣♣ *(5.36)* ♣♣♣

Every human personality is against every human personality like a war

♣♣♣ *(5.37)* ♣♣♣

Biggest goal of humans is trying to stay as humans

♣♣♣ *(5.38)* ♣♣♣

All human achievements are against nature

♣♣♣ *(5.39)* ♣♣♣

Humans are born to consume resources and live by statistics

♣♣♣ *(5.40)* ♣♣♣

Root cause of human unrest is they are seized by heart and mind

♣♣♣ *(5.41)* ♣♣♣

Human tranquillity and order is disturbed when there no bread

♣♣♣ *(5.42)* ♣♣♣

All great matters are conducted not above human nature

♣♣♣ *(5.43)* ♣♣♣

Humans are designed to endure more and enjoy less

♣♣♣ *(5.44)* ♣♣♣

Human perception is always confused to distinguish between what is good or evil

♣♣♣*(5.45)*♣♣♣

Human spirituality can't coexist with desires

♣♣♣*(5.46)*♣♣♣

Human nature follows imaginary things

♣♣♣*(5.47)*♣♣♣

There is nothing new in humans from wherever they are

♣♣♣*(5.48)*♣♣♣

Humans prefer excuse than remedy

♣♣♣*(5.49)*♣♣♣

Humans hate those they have hurt

♣♣♣*(5.50)*♣♣♣

All humans love what is good in them

♣♣♣*(5.51)*♣♣♣

Well performed human duty should be with duty discharged
with judicious human rights

♣♣♣*(5.52)*♣♣♣

Best people are made out of faults

♣♣♣*(5.53)*♣♣♣

Humans  are not ashamed

♣♣♣*(5.54)*♣♣♣

For maintaining world order prevention of human oppression is
more important than prevention of human sin

♣♣♣*(5.55)*♣♣♣

Human honestly and altruism makes people uncomfortable and
unhappy

♣♣♣*(5.56)*♣♣♣

Being human we can't ignore humanity

♣♣♣*(5.57)*♣♣♣

Human knowledge so much finite that can't even predict
happening in uncertainty

♣♣♣*(5.58)*♣♣♣

Man is bestowed with good and great strength that he don't
want

♣♣♣*(5.59)*♣♣♣

Keeping optimistic attitude of laughter at every situation
prevents you from weeping in life

♣♣♣ *(5.60)* ♣♣♣

Significance of man is his significance for universe

♣♣♣ *(5.61)* ♣♣♣

Man's world is world of necessity and freedom

♣♣♣ *(5.62)* ♣♣♣

Man's senses can ever fulfil satisfaction

♣♣♣ *(5.63)* ♣♣♣

For pleasure of life you should not repeat your moments

♣♣♣ *(5.64)* ♣♣♣

Humans are self annihilating in modern era with so called
modern

♣♣♣ *(5.65)* ♣♣♣

In this age you find only bad and worse people

♣♣♣ *(5.66)* ♣♣♣

Speculation of risk is alone unique to humans

♣♣♣ *(5.67)* ♣♣♣

Every human personality is against every human personality
like a war

♣♣♣ *(5.68)* ♣♣♣

Biggest goal of humans is trying to stay as humans

♣♣♣ *(5.69)* ♣♣♣

Humans are born to consume resources and live by statistics

♣♣♣ *(5.70)* ♣♣♣

Root cause of human unrest is they are seized by heart and
mind

♣♣♣ *(5.71)* ♣♣♣

Human tranquillity and order is disturbed when there no bread

♣♣♣ *(5.72)* ♣♣♣

Fables rule human life rather facts

♣♣♣ *(5.73)* ♣♣♣

Humans are designed to endure more and enjoy less

♣♣♣ *(5.74)* ♣♣♣

Human perception is always confused to distinguish between what is good or evil

♣♣♣(5.75)♣♣♣

Human spirituality can't coexist with desires

♣♣♣(5.76)♣♣♣

Human nature follows imaginary things

♣♣♣(5.77)♣♣♣

There is nothing new in humans from wherever they are

♣♣♣(5.78)♣♣♣

Humans those who seek from others like a beggars are true kings

♣♣♣(5.79)♣♣♣

Humans become sick by humans

♣♣♣(5.80)♣♣♣

No human is perfect

♣♣♣(5.81)♣♣♣

Humans are just like  links of a chain

♣♣♣(5.82)♣♣♣

Contradictions are inbuilt in humans

♣♣♣(5.83)♣♣♣

Humans cannot be confined

♣♣♣(5.84)♣♣♣

There is no easy walk to human freedom

♣♣♣(5.85)♣♣♣

Human flame of freedom can't be extinguished

♣♣♣(5.86)♣♣♣

Enemies of human freedom never argue or discuss just act against

♣♣♣(5.87)♣♣♣

Human freedom is more ambiguous and more abused

♣♣♣(5.88)♣♣♣

One's freedom can't be prescribed by others

♣♣♣(5.89)♣♣♣

Being alone is fundamental to human life

♣♣♣(5.90)♣♣♣

There is no winning in human affairs

♣♣♣*(5.91)*♣♣♣

Humans carry their human condition

♣♣♣*(5.92)*♣♣♣

Humans live and learn

♣♣♣*(5.93)*♣♣♣

Man is a measure of all things

♣♣♣*(5.94)*♣♣♣

Man can be justified by his sacrifice

♣♣♣*(5.95)*♣♣♣

Man is born free but he chains himself

♣♣♣*(5.96)*♣♣♣

Human  disorders are due to non perceived human capacity to experience pleasures and pains

♣♣♣*(5.97)*♣♣♣

Noblest human essence is spreading sweetness and showing direction of light

♣♣♣*(5.98)*♣♣♣

Majority of humans live in desperation

♣♣♣*(5.99)*♣♣♣

Constituents of modern human beings are diseases and impurities

♣♣♣*(5.100)*♣♣♣

Man's invisible man always demands ridiculous more

♣♣♣*(5.101)*♣♣♣

Human life is being content and acceptance

♣♣♣*(5.102)*♣♣♣

Since man is social animal politics are integral to him

♣♣♣*(5.103)*♣♣♣

Tendency of human impulses always aspire to achieve something beyond natural

♣♣♣*(5.104)*♣♣♣

Human are born neither good nor bad

♣♣♣*(5.105)*♣♣♣

Some humans being hosts some humans being guests

♣♣♣*(5.106)*♣♣♣
Humans possess natural affinity towards groups of alike

♣♣♣*(5.107)*♣♣♣
Humanity lost due to people either have sense of reality but no principles or have principles but are insane

♣♣♣*(5.108)*♣♣♣
Man in man is humanity

♣♣♣*(5.109)*♣♣♣
Human are expected to pay mandatory premium to their group for being social animal

♣♣♣*(5.110)*♣♣♣
Good human whatever he seeks in himself seeks in others

♣♣♣*(5.111)*♣♣♣
All humans are born without indecent within

♣♣♣*(5.112)*♣♣♣
Future of humans depends upon how he mixes colours in his perception of imaginary vision

♣♣♣*(5.113)*♣♣♣
Unused human power is greatest power

♣♣♣*(5.114)*♣♣♣
All humans are misfit with acquired good and bad from others. Only proportion changes from person to person

♣♣♣*(5.115)*♣♣♣
Essence of human goodness prevails forever

♣♣♣*(5.116)*♣♣♣
Those only will survive who never get carried away

♣♣♣*(5.117)*♣♣♣
Humans automatically find productivity tools

♣♣♣*(5.118)*♣♣♣
Every man possess beast in him only visible to some

♣♣♣*(5.119)*♣♣♣
Animals never kill for playing. Only humans torture humans for pleasure

♣♣♣*(5.120)*♣♣♣
Greatest thing on earth is human mind

♣♣♣(5.121)♣♣♣
Man is only intellectual visionary animal

♣♣♣(5.122)♣♣♣
Human endeavour undermines humanity

♣♣♣(5.123)♣♣♣
There are only two types of humans advisors and advise seekers

♣♣♣(5.124)♣♣♣
Mankind is central to everything but not individualism

♣♣♣(5.125)♣♣♣
Iteration to improves is natural to human beings

♣♣♣(5.126)♣♣♣
Man who destroyed man

♣♣♣(5.127)♣♣♣
Man is man by what he does

♣♣♣(5.128)♣♣♣
Human head is redundant if heart is right

♣♣♣(5.129)♣♣♣
Good made man as beautiful machine. Unfortunately man doesn't use it for work rather use it for cosmetic appearance

♣♣♣(5.130)♣♣♣
Man is rarely genuine but imitating

♣♣♣(5.131)♣♣♣
In modern era money centred world subordinate human centred world

♣♣♣(5.132)♣♣♣
Human ideas are patterns of values

♣♣♣(5.133)♣♣♣
Humanity is confused don't know where to go

♣♣♣(5.134)♣♣♣
Man is greatest miracle and greatest problem in the world

♣♣♣(5.135)♣♣♣
Salvation of mankind lies only in making everything for common good

♣♣♣(5.136)♣♣♣

Man tries to escape being human

♣♣♣*(5.137)*♣♣♣

Humans are so weak that it is impossible to be desire less

♣♣♣*(5.138)*♣♣♣

Humans indulge in irrational things for unlikely gains

♣♣♣*(5.139)*♣♣♣

In general humans are more foolish than wise

♣♣♣*(5.140)*♣♣♣

Any human who lives in reality is sure of achieving his goals

♣♣♣*(5.141)*♣♣♣

Humans are creatures of emotions with prejudice

♣♣♣*(5.142)*♣♣♣

All humans trys to avoid suffering and seeks only happiness

♣♣♣*(5.143)*♣♣♣

Human nature changes with geological surroundings

♣♣♣*(5.144)*♣♣♣

Human life is what he thinks else it passes by

♣♣♣*(5.145)*♣♣♣

Casual speech of humans give evidence against their own understanding

♣♣♣*(5.146)*♣♣♣

It is easy to destroy a man than defeating him

♣♣♣*(5.147)*♣♣♣

Consistency is against nature hence consistent people too can't survive

♣♣♣*(5.148)*♣♣♣

Humans are bestowed with too much capacity for taking things granted

♣♣♣*(5.149)*♣♣♣

Humanity is basically learned behaviour

♣♣♣

# 6.ANXIETY AND DEPRESSION

Almost everyone in this modern world is suffering from anxiety only some admit and some don't.

Every one out of three persons are suffering from symptoms of some sort of depression.  Our lifestyles  have become so hectic we don't have time to even think, act or rest. Whole life is mentally disturbed due to lifestyle.

Whether you agree or not anxiety and depression have become part of life and there is no other way than managing them.

We brings out some easy and useful Interesting Tips That Help Manage Anxiety and Depression.

These tips Helps to Remove Mental Toxins of Mind.

# 6.Anxiety and Depression

## *Contents*

♣♣♣*(6.1)*♣♣♣
## ARTIFICIAL WORLD

We live in a artificial and synthetic world. Our senses are lost in artificiality and they tend to forget very intent of their creation. Due to this sometimes our perception of senses becomes abnormal and biased. Our senses time to time need to be calibrated.  Best way to heal and rejuvenate our senses is re-establishing connection with nature and ecology.


♣♣♣*(6.2)*♣♣♣
## TOXINS

Toxins can be either mental toxins (mental behaviour of mind affecting chemistry of brain) or physical toxins (physical toxins present in the body affecting chemistry of brain resulting in change of minds mental thinking).


♣♣♣*(6.3)*♣♣♣
## TOXIN TYPES

Our body consists of physical toxins that are A)Internally generated toxins as a by-product of body's biological processes and B)external toxins entering into the body by ingestion and other modes. These toxins effect both our physical body and mind either directly or indirectly. Body and mind are interconnected but can't see them in isolation. Self control can consciously control your mind only up to it's limited ability but if accumulation of physical toxins in your body is beyond threshold they can forcefully alter your brain chemistry directly or indirectly affecting your mind.


♣♣♣*(6.4)*♣♣♣
## SOCIAL LIFE

God created humans as social animals. Human progress as well as dominance over flora and fauna is merely due to social collaboration and cooperation. Ancient times humans lived in groups. During medieval period humans lived in joint families until modern times. However modern industrial age forced migrations disintegrated joint families and converted joint families into nuclear families. As long as humans lived in groups and joint families they had others emotional support and caring. Due to artificial life and due to lack of others caring, modern humans started accumulation of mental toxins due to changed thinking.

### ♣♣♣(6.5)♣♣♣
## DETOXIFICATION

Complete detoxification of human means detoxification of mind, body as well as his environment.

### ♣♣♣(6.6)♣♣♣
## ENVIRONMENT

For lakhs of years as animal humans lived naturally in environment.  Hence environment in which Humans live has profound affect on his mind and body. Environment in which Humans lived is engraved in human genes. Environment in which human lives influences accumulation of physical toxins by affecting biological processes of the body and also influences accumulation of mental toxins by affecting mind.

### ♣♣♣(6.7)♣♣♣
## SELFISHNESS

Ancient human became modern human by living in groups and joint families and collective thinking for common good. However due to circumstances modern human being thinking is individualistic and selfish. Modern humans have problems in human to human relationships due to clash of interests for common good versus individual interests. Since modern human is individualistic and selfish whenever he is under disadvantaged condition in human to human interactions his mental trauma and suffering is too much creating tons of mental toxins.

♣♣♣*(6.8)*♣♣♣
# RELATIONSHIPS

We all live with ego. If someone doesn't accept your requirement and says NO, you will never come back to him again. You will take his view a permanent and you will develop enmity and bitterness with that relationship affecting your mind.  People never the same, people do change with time and circumstances. Recall your relationships and friends and observe their  chronological personality changes, surely you will realise the fact. Humans relationships will never have same dynamics hence you can try after some time with same person.

♣♣♣*(6.9)*♣♣♣
# PROBLEMS

Life is full of problems to be solved whether it is personal or professional. This is fact of life. Whenever you are stuck with problem, in a heavy situation, bring humour to serious situations. This relaxes and rejuvenates your mind and makes it creative and gives breakthrough.

♣♣♣*(6.10)*♣♣♣
# ARGUMENT

Most of the people are stuck in endless arguments trying to enforce their point of view. In this process they get mentally disturbed resulting in accumulation of mental toxins. Please realise whether you accept or not truth will always prevails. The root cause of the problem is everyone rather addressing the problem tries to attack individual ego. Though there may be real solution to the problem, however there is a problem of acceptance by all due to adversely affected some parties. Hence ego clash do occurs between all. Best thing to avoid confrontation is to find a solution in between real solution to solution for common good.

♣♣♣*(6.11)*♣♣♣
## CONTROL OF EMOTIONS

When you are loaded with physical toxins and mental toxins, even normal small small interventions with your personality can trigger uncontrollable emotional response from you. Be cautious, remember, you have to take responsibility for your uncontrollable emotions. You must face reaction consequences of others action who faced your triggered heat. Subsequently you will regret your behaviour life time. You have to exercise some restraint, whenever trigger occurs count one to hundred numbers. All triggers persist only few seconds, during that time your mind is bypassed. All you need to do is delay your response by few seconds. On the other side if others are emotional don't consider their statements.

♣♣♣*(6.12)*♣♣♣
## APPROVAL OF OTHERS

Since humans are social animals they always seek consciously or unconsciously approval of others. This is a embedded logic in humans by nature. Others disapproval causes agony in humans. Realise the fact human behaviour is natural and remember you can't control others actions, however you can be mindful and can control your reactions.

♣♣♣*(6.13)*♣♣♣
## SELF REFLECTION

Modern lifestyle is so hectic and busy that makes you more mechanical like a robot. You will not be in a position to use your mind or heart effectively and efficiently. Self reflection is essential to regenerate your mind and heart to make them productive. Time to time detach yourself from your surroundings and leave space for self reflection and feeling in a calm environment.

♣♣♣*(6.14)*♣♣♣

## NULCLEAR FAMILIES

When humans started living as nuclear families from joint families they became individualistic and selfish. Due to lack of others emotional support they started indulging in self talk and comparing themselves with others. They lost ability to think for common good and good for others. Modern humans don't think everyone is unique and lost the ability assess self-worth and stared indulging in negative self talk. Imaginary feelings of lack of self worth is the main reason for creation of mental toxins.  Let go pessimistic self talk. Feel good about self. It is not that easy to let self remove self talk, just replace it with constructive thoughts.

♣♣♣*(6.15)*♣♣♣
## SUPPORTIVE PEOPLE

Since we are social beings our well-being and growth depends upon people who surrounds us. Always be with supportive and like minded people. You don't exist individually without others. You can't do anything without others. Without others it creates mental toxins.

♣♣♣*(6.16)*♣♣♣
## SLEEP

Sleep consumes half of our life. That shows importance of sleep held by human designer i.e.  god. Sleep regenerates your body and mind. Adhere to convenient routines for sleep. Benefits of sleep are beyond human comprehension. Sleep repairs and rejuvenates body and mind. Sleep enables unconscious self reflection of mind and heart and gives creative solution to unsolved problems. Sleep removes mental toxins.

♣♣♣*(6.17)*♣♣♣
## NEGATIVE THINKING

Life is full of opportunities whether you want to know or not. However most people shut this window of opportunities due to negative thinking and attitude resulting due to mental toxins. Be optimistic, replace the word I can't with I can. When you are optimistic, opportunities comes your way.

### ♣♣♣(6.18)♣♣♣
## SELF IMPORTANCE
Since we always seek others approval we are sensitive to others and unconsciously keep others above us even though they don't deserve. In this process we forget our own importance and we are hijacked and controlled by others. The clash of our own intuitions and others wants creates mind conflicts resulting in mental toxins.  Make self first priority in life this is as important as your existence and to get rid of mental toxins.

### ♣♣♣(6.19)♣♣♣
## NATURE OF LIFE
Life is never a straight road, journey takes you through all sorts of roads, you can't drive in same way in all types of roads, you need to adjust your ride, then only you will reach your destination. Your behaviour must be like water, try to be flexible rather being too rigid or too serious in life. Being rigid results in creation of mental toxins.

### ♣♣♣(6.20)♣♣♣
## INTUTION
You will be energetic and thriving when you listen to your intuition and follow your nature. When you do so you create a magnetic you shielding any mental toxin  tries to enter you.

### ♣♣♣(6.21)♣♣♣
## CHOICE
Every moment of life is a choice. Any choice has risk of going fifty-fifty right or wrong. Hence never regret consequences of selecting a choice. Just wait for next opportunity of choice to

correct again. Only god only can make correct and right choice. No human has that ability. Be judicious and consciously make choices within limitations of your circumstances. Never accumulate mental toxins by over thinking about consequences.

### ♣♠♣ *(6.22)* ♣♠♣
## TRUTHFULLNESS

As long as you aren't true to self and others you live not you rather you try and pretend to be other. Difference between real personality and fictitious personality creates mental toxins. If you are authentic and realistic then only you can elevate your health.  If you do so you won't stress your mind and you will be natural behaving naturally.

### ♣♠♣ *(6.23)* ♣♠♣
## NATURE OF PESSIMISM

Negativity is the main mental toxin of mind. Pessimism is a seed & behaves like a exponential triggered chain reaction cascading and propagating like ripples in water. Negativity is a closed loop continuously repeating and creating ever increasing ripples.

### ♣♠♣ *(6.24)* ♣♠♣
## DETOXING MIND

First step to detox your mind is you have to break negativity ever repeating loop chain. For that you have to choose few rhyming words like a mantra and start repeatedly pronouncing these rhyming words like a loop.  Once you do this repeated rhyming automatically you will replace your negative thinking loop.

### ♣♠♣ *(6.25)* ♣♠♣
## DETOXING & FOCUS

Second step to detox mind is stop thinking. Continue with your repeated rhyming and simultaneously try to focus on your breathing or externally on any imaginary focal point. Slowly increase depth of your focus from macro level to micro level until you have created a condition of unique absolute thoughtlessness or stillness or tranquillity.

### ♣♣♣ *(6.26)* ♣♣♣
## DETOXING & THOUGHTS

Third step to detox after coming out of stillness, replace all your thinking with only positive and constructive thoughts.

### ♣♣♣ *(6.27)* ♣♣♣
## DETOXING & MINDFULNESS

Fourth step to detox is being and staying mindful, whatever you do only thinking of present moment and living in the present.

### ♣♣♣ *(6.28)* ♣♣♣
## DETOXING & BREATHING

Fifth step to detox is  practice any one type of breathing exercise for few  minutes daily  like pranayamam. This will tranquilize your mind and recharges. There are lot of scientific and non scientific breathing exercises available openly follow any one of them. These breathing exercises you can do at any place or posture of your convenience. Breathing exercise helps to remain mindful, focused and energetic.

### ♣♣♣ *(6.29)* ♣♣♣
## ARTIFICIAL WORLD

One of the direct and indirect affect of negativity loop thinking is progressive and exponential accumulation of toxins in the body.

### ♣♣♣ *(6.30)* ♣♣♣
## NUTS & OMEGA3

Nuts and seeds repairs as well as keeps your mind healthy due to presence of omega3 fatty acids and other nutrients.

However you have to consume limited quantity daily. Avoid raw nuts and seeds and consume only after soaking them in water over night. You can change nut types periodically.

### ♣♣♣(6.31)♣♣♣
## SPIRITUAL DIMENSION

Add spiritual component to your life.  Spirituality gives you clarity, confidence and mental peace. Spirituality is a necessity for humans. Goodness of spirituality is proven for thousands of years. Spirituality is one of the very good detoxing antidote and it enables being mindful.

### ♣♣♣(6.32)♣♣♣
## SELF REALISATION

Mental peace comes from true self realisation. Self realisation is true state of life. Doubts are mental agitation. Doubts are cleared by being mindful. Doubt creates mental toxins.

### ♣♣♣(6.33)♣♣♣
## PROCRASTINATION

Unfulfilling jobs can cause mental toxins. You need to be systematic, organised to do anything. People indulge in procrastination due to imaginary fears rather facts.  Most of our fears are like mirages. Many lack only in initiation.

### ♣♣♣(6.34)♣♣♣
## MEDITATION

Many forms of Meditation is available. You can choose any one of them that suits you. Meditation generates life energy and force.

### ♣♣♣(6.35)♣♣♣
## CALMNESS

Keep cool and clam in everyday of life. This restraint is essential in hectic modern life. You can't change or make things happen overnight. Things takes their own time whether you feel for them or not.

### ♣♣♣(6.36)♣♣♣
## PHYSICAL EXERCISES

At least 30 minutes gentle physical exercises are required for body to keep brain hormones secretions healthy. At least do some gentle exercises regularly like walking or some yoga exercises. Hormones help to maintain brains chemistry.

### ♣♣♣(6.37)♣♣♣
## KIDS

When you play with kids are pets that relaxes you and detoxes your mental toxins. They are playful and innocent soothing your heart and mind with deep impact.

### ♣♣♣(6.38)♣♣♣
## OTHER ACTIVITIES

When you are disturbed divert yourself and glue to a favourite TV program or go far a bicycle ride or swimming.

### ♣♣♣(6.39)♣♣♣
## WOMEN

When compared to men, women are better at handling emotions as they care and raise children. Women are natural emotional dampeners. Whenever you are loaded with mental toxins spend some time with women in your life talking.

### ♣♣♣(6.40)♣♣♣
## SPORTS

Playing some outdoor sporting activities will help you to detox mental toxins.

### ♣♣♣(6.41)♣♣♣
## REFERENCES

Ayurveda ancient wisdom for wellbeing by GeetaVara

# 7.OBESITY AND GOOD DIET

Transition to modern world made world services work oriented without much physical activity or exercise due invention of machines and equipment of comfort.

People are more and more drinking, boozing and wining and habituated to unnatural fast foods and desserts.

Every seven out of ten persons are obscene or over weight due to over eating of unhealthy food habits and lack of exercise.

Girls and Women cherish and nourish all those who are near and dear to them. They are the foundation to every family of every country and there is no exception.

Entire family wellbeing depends upon girls and women who care for. However due to lack of basic understanding there is shortfall in their caring.

# 7.Obesity and Good Diet

## Contents

♣♣♣*(7.1)*♣♣♣
# NATURE AND LIFESTYLE

Observe and learn from nature. Nature made supreme rule, there is no exception we have to obey. Those who followed ancient cultures of natural living only surviving through all modern revolutions and evolutions.

♣♣♣*(7.2)*♣♣♣
# ABILITY OF NATURE

What nature can do is limitless, only it's use is limited upto your understanding. Nature is incredibly smart and intelligent.

♣♣♣*(7.3)*♣♣♣
# NATURAL LIVING

Nature is supreme force. Everything that exists in nature must obey natural laws including flora and fauna. Nature knows only random order. Each constituent of flora and fauna has unique biorhythm. As long as fauna obeys nature's natural order it flourishes without any disorder or affect. Nature has unique ability of self repairing of its constituents and bouncing back to natural order. When fauna lives in equilibrium with nature it is perfect, it's growth is normal, it thrives and rejuvenates. Nature knows no discrimination. When fauna consumes what is grown seasonally in its vicinity, it's nourishment is perfect, well balanced and faunas body gains maximum benefit.
As long as you live naturally with nature you can be self healed by nature. Natural living with nature prevents disorders.

♣♣♣*(7.4)*♣♣♣
# UNBALANCE

Surrender to nature. Embrace life as it flows naturally. When you try to deviate from your path disorder or disturbance starts to creep in. Your well being depends upon your mind, heart, body, soul and their association with nature as well as universe. Nature is you, you are the nature. You are the creation of

Nature. No force can stop influence of natural force. Ultimately everything has to yield it to. Your disorder grows as you try to shift from naturally living life style to synthetic & artificial life style.

### ♣♣♣(7.5)♣♣♣
## ANIMAL AND HUMANS DIFFERENCE

Other than humans, animals eats by what is given by nature lives by what is provided by nature and are rarely diseased. Even meat eating animals know how to naturally live for maintaining their body, they observe intermittently rigorous fasting. Unfortunately meat eating humans knows only eating and never fasting. That is the main cause of body imbalance.

### ♣♣♣(7.6)♣♣♣
## FOOD

Food gives you universal experience. What you depends upon what you eat. Good digestion depends on good conscience but not on good appetite.

### ♣♣♣(7.7)♣♣♣
## FOOD KNOWLEDGE

Learning principles and knowledge about food is not compulsory to remain healthy. However if you do physical and mental hard work you will be surely remain healthy.

### ♣♣♣(7.8)♣♣♣
## FOOD QUANTITY

Short meal with few dishes will be a perfect meal. Good dinner brings everyone hearts together. Sharing eating increases its pleasure. Wholesome food gives more nourishment than mess. Merely handful of food items sufficient for our daily food allowances.

### ♣♣♣(7.9)♣♣♣

# FOOD IMPORTANCE

Without food your mind and heart won't function. When you consume right diet you don't need any medicine. When you consume wrong diet even medicine is ineffective.

*♣♣♣(7.10)♣♣♣*

## LOCAL FOOD

Local food protects you from local climate. Use local fruits and vegetables of the season.

*♣♣♣(7.11)♣♣♣*

## FOOD & HEALTH

Food affects our emotions as much as it affects our physical body. You are unique, hence your diet should be specific to you. There can't be common ideal diet for all.

*♣♣♣(7.12)♣♣♣*

## BALANCED FOOD

Balanced diet nourishes, builds and repairs every cell in our body. Knowing when to eat, when to not is important for having healthy digestive system.

*♣♣♣(7.13)♣♣♣*

## SEASONAL FOOD

Constituent elements of nature changes with seasons so do the balance of your body. Hence you need to alter food items consumption as per seasonal foods items availability.

*♣♣♣(7.14)♣♣♣*

## NATURAL FOOD

Nutrients will give real benefits to body only when you take them in their natural food sources form rather using supplements.

*♣♣♣(7.15)♣♣♣*

# STORED FOOD

Avoid frozen, cold stored and cold food items. Don't consume carbonated food items.

## ♣♣♣*(7.16)*♣♣♣
# INDIGESTION

Antidote for indigestion is using food that is pungent in nature like ginger, garlic, black pepper etc

## ♣♣♣*(7.17)*♣♣♣
# FRUITS

Fruits are easy to digest and assimilate by the body. However you need to consume limited amount of fruit servings daily. Sour, citrus and unripe fruits can imbalance the body.

## ♣♣♣*(7.18)*♣♣♣
# FOOD AND HUNGER AND THIRST

Our sensation and feeling mistakes and can't distinguish inbetween thirst and hunger. Drinking little warm water 25 minutes before meals can help prevent overeating.

## ♣♣♣*(7.19)*♣♣♣
# OVEREATING AND DIGESTION

Avoid overeating and overdoing. Overeating, frequently eating, untimely eating contributes to bodys imbalance. Constant feasting weakens digestive energy and reduces detoxification ability of the body. Snaking inbetween meals is an invitation for toxins. During lunch time digestion is strongest. Hence, heavy meals must be consumed during lunch time.

## ♣♣♣*(7.20)*♣♣♣
# JUNK FOOD

Your body craves for pleasure of sugar. By default hunger will pull you towards food items either you are habituated or addicted. When you are hunger and attracted to junk food, pause a while and drink a glass of water and try to divert your attention towards others things like nature. When you detox your body automatically your body stops craving for junk food and strats liking for healthy food.

### ♣♣♣ *(7.21)* ♣♣♣
## VEGETARIAN DIET

Plant based diet takes away what aggravates the body, gives rest to bodys immune system and enables it to heal naturally. Limit consumption of root vegetables. It is advisable to have vegetarian meals in the evening. To the possible extent prefer vegetarian meals all times.

### ♣♣♣ *(7.22)* ♣♣♣
## FOOD COMPATIBILITY

Avoid any food that causes any kind of negative effect on the body. Normal non suitable foods cause negative effects in different ways  like diarrhoea, congestion and running nose, constipation, skin issues, inflammation,  food sensitivities.

### ♣♣♣ *(7.23)* ♣♣♣
## FOODS TO AVOID

Refined food can cause blood sugar level fluctuations. Avoid red meat and desserts.

### ♣♣♣ *(7.24)* ♣♣♣
## NUTS

Nuts, seeds and whole foods keeps you energetic. Nuts must be consumed by soaking overnight in water for more effectiveness and efficiency.

### ♣♣♣ *(7.25)* ♣♣♣
## COOKING

Good  hygiene whether it is personal or surroundings is important. Steam cooked food items are more compatible and easily digested by body. Boiling milk prior to drinking makes milk more digestible. If you roast in oil some essential oils sensitive to heat can breakdown to toxins.

### ♣♣♣*(7.26)*♣♣♣
## WAY TO EAT

You should take food in calm and relaxed environment. Enjoy every bit of food by focused chewing and sensing. Eat only up to half of your stomach capacity. Minimise water mealtime. Drink warm/hot water. Maintain and follow specified meal timings.

### ♣♣♣*(7.27)*♣♣♣
## TIMING

Eating breakfast as late as possible and dinner as early as possible is beneficial to body. Skipping breakfast may help sometimes normal persons. What you eat, how you eat and when you eat decides your digestive ability. Eating when not hungry, consuming non compatible combinations, stress, irregular eating timings, can imbalance your digestive system.

### ♣♣♣*(7.28)*♣♣♣
## LIVER

Your liver is a chemical factory for the body. When you don't care your food, your liver is first to get affected. Beyond certain threshold irreversible changes can occur in liver. Liver is the most important vital organ for life having far reaching cascading consequences.

### ♣♣♣*(7.29)*♣♣♣
## INTESTINES

Good Conditions of Intestines is important for vitality and immunity of body. Restoration of good intestine Conditions is an important step for body's Detoxification process. Unnatural life style ends up changing our intestines in a negative ways.

### ♣♣♣*(7.30)*♣♣♣
## LIFESTYLE

Don't follow sedentary life style sit less and move more. Every moment is a choice, your choice to live a healthy lifestyle. By adapted lifestyle either you author own health or disease. Remember lifestyle change takes time, have patience. Due to modern lifestyle no one's body functions optimally anymore.

### ♣♣♣*(7.31)*♣♣♣
## MODERN LIFESTYLE

Comfortable modern lifestyle unknowingly stresses our bodies with dormant consequences. We gained few comforts and many problems with modern lifestyle. We all prefer artificial approach when compared to natural approach w.r.t. living style. We are so much habituated, we take life as it is today for granted. Modern lifestyle adversely affected our body's natural rhythm and created constant state of unbalance. Industrial progress forced humans to change their lifestyle.

### ♣♣♣*(7.32)*♣♣♣
## ROUTINES

Adhere to convenient routines for sleep, exercise and diet. Your body is your temple, respect and care it.

### ♣♣♣*(7.33)*♣♣♣
## TOXINS AND BODY

Endogenous toxins are generated in the body due to toxic waste products of body cellular metabolism. Exogenous toxins coming to body that are foreign to body which behaves like pollutants or poisons. Body is damaged due to substantial amount of toxin accumulated due to modern lifestyle. Modern lifestyle made us to be vulnerable  to constant bombardment by toxins. Accumulated toxicity throws body out of balance and it interferes with intelligence of body's self organising ability.

Accumulated toxicity throws body out of balance and it interferes with intelligence of body's self organising ability. Accumulation of internal,  external toxins are reflected as toxic thoughts and toxic emotions. Our bodies are not capable of meeting today's demand for constant and continuous high level of detoxification inorder to keep it self managed.

### ♣♣♣(7.34)♣♣♣
## DETOXIFICATION

Detoxifying is restoring body's natural ability of self healing. Detoxification means detoxifying physical body, sensors, environment, relationships as well as emotions. When you are detoxifying body if you still consume toxic food that is affecting your detoxifying process you can't achieve detoxifying. Spices useful to expel toxins are hot water, herbal teas, ginger, cinnamon, fennel, black pepper etc.

### ♣♣♣(7.35)♣♣♣
## DISEASE

Alignment is experiencing overload of toxins. Breaking laws and rules of nature creates diseases. When equilibrium of natural order is disturbed disease will start due to unbalanced condition.

### ♣♣♣(7.36)♣♣♣
## DISEASE RECOVERY

You need to restore supplies of what is lacking in the body by observing and with manual intervention. Choosing suitable diet is important for treatment of disease. Your body knows how to self repair, restore, heal, cure and rejuvenate, only you have to create suitable conditions. Practice of using plants for medical purpose exits in all countries of the world. There is no demarcation between medical plants and plant based foods. Altering to plant based food with properties that help in restoring body's natural balance will be helpful. Body demands rest for supporting self-healing process. Sometimes if it is too essential it forces you to take rest. Process of healing is built-in the body. Your doctor only helps that process. Health and restoration of health is unique to individual. You write your health.

### ♣♣♣(7.37)♣♣♣
## AYURVEDA

Ayurveda and Chinese medicine techniques proven for centuries for their effectiveness. Ayurveda is effective in eliminating root cause of disease and rejuvenating body.

### ♣♣♣(7.38)♣♣♣
## FASTING

Fasting starts consuming own resources of body. Body has priorities for cells for allowing to self consume. Diseased cells will be allowed to be consumed on first priority when compared to healthy cells. This is the reason for self healing on fasting for most of common diseases. Intermittently fasting is good to rejuvenate body. However first time you should do fasting under expert advice. Process of fasting commences after twelve hours of last meal. For normal persons beneficial changes can occurs 24 hrs of fasting. However it depends upon nature of individual body.

### ♣♣♣(7.39)♣♣♣
## FOOD DURING FASTING

Effective fasting food is liquid based like fruit, vegetables juices. Fasting does not mean completely keeping away from food. Fasting is keeping your body on simplified and reduced diet suiting to the nature of your body.

### ♣♣♣(7.40)♣♣♣
## REFERENCES
Ayurveda Books

# 8.POLITICS AND GOVERNANCE

In politics there are no friends or enemies, only permutations and combinations for opportunities of power. It is impossible to predict anything.

A Honest true politician is capable of eradicating human suffering and creating a momentum of sustained human development in a society there by uplifting society.

Understanding real politics and governance is very difficult due to intrinsic and extrinsic factors involved.

We have Presented here 243 nos of TIPS about basics and important properties of politics and governance in a very simple way.

♣♣♣(8.1)♣♣♣
Practitioners of politics are mostly by unlike
♣♣♣(8.2)♣♣♣
Political education bestows knowledge of human nature
♣♣♣(8.3)♣♣♣
Liberalism is directing others spending
♣♣♣(8.4)♣♣♣
For survival man had to become social animal. Since he became
social animal he has become political animal automatically
♣♣♣(8.5)♣♣♣
Politics is a wild sport
♣♣♣(8.6)♣♣♣
Politics is not an exact
♣♣♣(8.7)♣♣♣
Politics is not a task of religion
♣♣♣(8.8)♣♣♣
8.8)Politics can never make anyone happy
♣♣♣(8.9)♣♣♣
Politicians opinion is ever changing never remains the same
♣♣♣(8.10)♣♣♣
There is nothing like final in politics
♣♣♣(8.11)♣♣♣
A group is perpetually corrupted by personality character
♣♣♣(8.12)♣♣♣
Political leader never believes what he says
♣♣♣(8.13)♣♣♣
Honesty and politics never coexist
♣♣♣(8.14)♣♣♣
8Politicians can promise impossible as possible
♣♣♣(8.15)♣♣♣
Politicians are the same all over irrespective of individual
attributes
♣♣♣(8.16)♣♣♣
Conservatism is choice in-between using experience and
assuming risk new

♣♣♣(8.17)♣♣♣

Politicians are capable of taking and acting even before knowing

♣♣♣(8.18)♣♣♣

Politics is war. War is politics without victimization or with victimization

♣♣♣(8.19)♣♣♣

Political speeches and writings are largely in the defence of lacking

♣♣♣(8.20)♣♣♣

True politicians act don't react

♣♣♣(8.21)♣♣♣

Politicians never lose temper whatever may be the pressure on them

♣♣♣(8.22)♣♣♣

Unhappiness  is the root cause for politics

♣♣♣(8.23)♣♣♣

All politics are due to biased polarized attitude of majority

♣♣♣(8.24)♣♣♣

Politics is a forceful disturbance of majority for gain of few

♣♣♣(8.25)♣♣♣

Politicians knows pulse of public. They are ahead of public opinion

♣♣♣(8.26)♣♣♣

A radical man is one without any foundation

♣♣♣(8.27)♣♣♣

Conservatism is confused forward and backward oscillation swings

♣♣♣(8.28)♣♣♣

Politician known's everything without knowing anything

♣♣♣(8.29)♣♣♣

Politics are instantaneous no preparation is necessary

♣♣♣(8.30)♣♣♣

Politics is a synthetic culture created by few that prevents people from taking part in affairs concern to them

♣♣♣*(8.31)*♣♣♣

Politics gather strangers together

♣♣♣*(8.32)*♣♣♣

Promise of prosperity is always first promise in politics

♣♣♣*(8.33)*♣♣♣

Capitalism recreates out of revolution

♣♣♣*(8.34)*♣♣♣

Capitalism never known's how much good done by those who enjoyed freedom and who affected to commerce for the public good

♣♣♣*(8.35)*♣♣♣

Communism is a process to make unequal things equal things

♣♣♣*(8.36)*♣♣♣

People view communism sceptical due to its violent associations in different parts of the world

♣♣♣*(8.37)*♣♣♣

Communist economy keeps people desperate

♣♣♣*(8.38)*♣♣♣

Democracy may be the way to select few able by for many incompetent

♣♣♣*(8.39)*♣♣♣

Democracy always tries to prove how unfit others are

♣♣♣*(8.40)*♣♣♣

Democracy is persuading others in your worst way with your honey words

♣♣♣*(8.41)*♣♣♣

Ambassador is designed to lie or deceit for the good of his represented entity

♣♣♣*(8.42)*♣♣♣

Diplomacy is a cold war

♣♣♣*(8.43)*♣♣♣

Freedom is essence of life

♣♣♣*(8.44)*♣♣♣

Liberty is limited to do legally permitted everything

♣♣♣*(8.45)*♣♣♣

If unchecked many crime can be committed under mask of
liberty

♣♣♣*(8.46)*♣♣♣

Unlimited freedom is dangerous

♣♣♣*(8.47)*♣♣♣

Freedom less people fight for what they long for

♣♣♣*(8.48)*♣♣♣

Liberty is bestowed only with judicious vigilance

♣♣♣*(8.49)*♣♣♣

There are two types of people 1)borne to rule and 2)born to
advise

♣♣♣*(8.50)*♣♣♣

Liberty gives natural progress

♣♣♣*(8.51)*♣♣♣

People feel government is good if it provides most and governs
least

♣♣♣*(8.52)*♣♣♣

Government governance should reflect honesty

♣♣♣*(8.53)*♣♣♣

Law cannot be administered without  government

♣♣♣*(8.54)*♣♣♣

Hardest task for politician is to know what is right

♣♣♣*(8.55)*♣♣♣

Power is bestowed to discharge not only for good, otherwise
also as needs require

♣♣♣*(8.56)*♣♣♣

Leader either fulfils or exploits hopes of his people

♣♣♣*(8.57)*♣♣♣

Power and corruption are twin siblings

♣♣♣*(8.58)*♣♣♣

Most great men had to be bad men

♣♣♣*(8.59)*♣♣♣

Unchecked power tends to be abused

♣♣♣*(8.60)*♣♣♣

In the dictionary of power the word joy do not exist

♣♣♣ *(8.61)* ♣♣♣

Possessing good knowledge without power to utilize gives psychological  pain to one

♣♣♣ *(8.62)* ♣♣♣

All tends to desire power either formally or informally

♣♣♣ *(8.63)* ♣♣♣

Power desires more power. Its ever unfulfilled passion

♣♣♣ *(8.64)* ♣♣♣

Political power seeds out of reaction to freedom

♣♣♣ *(8.65)* ♣♣♣

You cannot be master of all

♣♣♣ *(8.66)* ♣♣♣

Power is a contagious disease

♣♣♣ *(8.67)* ♣♣♣

Power to survive love for power is must

♣♣♣ *(8.68)* ♣♣♣

God is only highest power

♣♣♣ *(8.69)* ♣♣♣

Revolutions seeds out of series of government faults

♣♣♣ *(8.70)* ♣♣♣

Participation in revolution is treated as enemy

♣♣♣ *(8.71)* ♣♣♣

Revolution  have no personal bondage except its purpose

♣♣♣ *(8.72)* ♣♣♣

For some revolution is fulltime of occupation

♣♣♣ *(8.73)* ♣♣♣

Desperate problems require desperate cure

♣♣♣ *(8.74)* ♣♣♣

Power treats a man who says no as rebel

♣♣♣ *(8.75)* ♣♣♣

Socialism and humanity coexist

♣♣♣ *(8.76)* ♣♣♣

Socialism is solution for socio economic system problems

♣♣♣ *(8.77)* ♣♣♣

Power has no friends

♣♣♣*(8.78)*♣♣♣
Power is above law
♣♣♣*(8.79)*♣♣♣
Democracy is the theory
♣♣♣*(8.80)*♣♣♣
Only enforcement of justices makes democracy a reality
♣♣♣*(8.81)*♣♣♣
Liberty is the spirit that exists in the heart of men and women
♣♣♣*(8.82)*♣♣♣
You cannot govern without others consent to be governed
♣♣♣*(8.83)*♣♣♣
Moral government is felt as worst government
♣♣♣*(8.84)*♣♣♣
Governments exists to protect rights of underprivileged
♣♣♣*(8.85)*♣♣♣
Democracy cannot tolerate authority
♣♣♣*(8.86)*♣♣♣
Justice is moral mandatory obligation
♣♣♣*(8.87)*♣♣♣
Test for leadership is ability to identify incipient problem
♣♣♣*(8.88)*♣♣♣
Power is like lightening that injures without prior warning
♣♣♣*(8.89)*♣♣♣
Power automatically comes from sincere service
♣♣♣*(8.90)*♣♣♣
Power is opium
♣♣♣*(8.91)*♣♣♣
Economic freedom is essential for achieving political freedom
♣♣♣*(8.92)*♣♣♣
Man only consumes
♣♣♣*(8.93)*♣♣♣
Communism and prohibition coexist
♣♣♣*(8.94)*♣♣♣
Acts and laws under are good only as we make progress under
them

♣♣♣*(8.95)*♣♣♣
Acts and laws under constitution are promised commitment for good governance
♣♣♣*(8.96)*♣♣♣
Democracy is difficult to govern
♣♣♣*(8.97)*♣♣♣
reedom is natural craving of the mind
♣♣♣*(8.98)*♣♣♣
Freedom is not deliverance
♣♣♣*(8.99)*♣♣♣
Economic freedom is prior requirement for real freedom
♣♣♣*(8.100)*♣♣♣
Demand for freedom is contagious
♣♣♣*(8.101)*♣♣♣
Freedom is freedom of moral
♣♣♣*(8.102)*♣♣♣
True liberty is sustained independence
♣♣♣*(8.103)*♣♣♣
True character is known only under freedom
♣♣♣*(8.104)*♣♣♣
Whatever may be the form of government everyone expects better living conditions
♣♣♣*(8.105)*♣♣♣
Government own conveniences are expressed as philosophies
♣♣♣*(8.106)*♣♣♣
Public confidence is a reflection of government performance
♣♣♣*(8.107)*♣♣♣
It is very easy to accuse imperfections
♣♣♣*(8.108)*♣♣♣
Efficiency requires some sort of dictatorship
♣♣♣*(8.109)*♣♣♣
Democracy is rendered meaningless if justice is delayed
♣♣♣*(8.110)*♣♣♣
A leader is a manager in hope
♣♣♣*(8.111)*♣♣♣

Politics are as good as war

♣♣♣(8.112)♣♣♣

Political action is highest responsibility

♣♣♣(8.113)♣♣♣

Politicians never live in private upto their public promises

♣♣♣(8.114)♣♣♣

Great harm cannot be done if the tenure of the office is short

♣♣♣(8.115)♣♣♣

Public opinion is unsafe to ignore

♣♣♣(8.116)♣♣♣

Public opinion is a thermometer for satisfaction

♣♣♣(8.117)♣♣♣

All rules do have exceptions

♣♣♣(8.118)♣♣♣

Economic insecurity seizes ones liberty

♣♣♣(8.119)♣♣♣

Economists will never reach conclusion

♣♣♣(8.120)♣♣♣

Socialism fails due to economic reality

♣♣♣(8.121)♣♣♣

Stability of state comes from reality of equality under constitution

♣♣♣(8.122)♣♣♣

We are born unequal. Equality is the requirement of human existence. Nature has no equality

♣♣♣(8.123)♣♣♣

Freedom can only give you peace

♣♣♣(8.124)♣♣♣

Feeling of power is self-care

♣♣♣(8.125)♣♣♣

Feeling of liberty is love of others

♣♣♣(8.126)♣♣♣

You have to be tough to make government efficient

♣♣♣(8.127)♣♣♣

Government is supposed to represent facts

♣♣♣*(8.128)*♣♣♣
Order of society depends on justice
♣♣♣*(8.129)*♣♣♣
Mercy bears more fruits than punishment
♣♣♣*(8.130)*♣♣♣
Law is a order for common good
♣♣♣*(8.131)*♣♣♣
You are capable of accomplishing more than your power
♣♣♣*(8.132)*♣♣♣
Unchecked power corrupts
♣♣♣*(8.133)*♣♣♣
Intentionally ignoring facts is part of practical politics
♣♣♣*(8.134)*♣♣♣
Unlimited freedom without law compliance will make one unpredictable and uncontrollable
♣♣♣*(8.135)*♣♣♣
Human decisions are not based on mathematical reasoning alone
♣♣♣*(8.136)*♣♣♣
Politics are exempted from explanation
♣♣♣*(8.137)*♣♣♣
Government exists to establish values by changing society
♣♣♣*(8.138)*♣♣♣
Individually untrue persons cannot be true in public
♣♣♣*(8.139)*♣♣♣
Mutual bonding undermines common good
♣♣♣*(8.140)*♣♣♣
Defeat with war is too expensive than defeat without war
♣♣♣*(8.141)*♣♣♣
Everyone  has to do what they  are supposed to do for enabling governance system
♣♣♣*(8.142)*♣♣♣
When to not talk is more important in politics
♣♣♣*(8.143)*♣♣♣
You have to judge man by ability to listen right

♣♣♣*(8.144)*♣♣♣
Civil servant is a complying pendulum to yes
or no at discretion to power
♣♣♣*(8.145)*♣♣♣
Political party is a organized opinion based on consensus
♣♣♣*(8.146)*♣♣♣
Politics creates deception to believe everyone had big
advantage though not
♣♣♣*(8.147)*♣♣♣
For government to work constitution must work
♣♣♣*(8.148)*♣♣♣
8Leader normally resorts to group opinion only when he can't
take individual decision
♣♣♣*(8.149)*♣♣♣
People in power are pleased with small gratitude's rather big
favours
♣♣♣*(8.150)*♣♣♣
In politics sometimes you have to defend what is right and lose
♣♣♣*(8.151)*♣♣♣
People are preoccupied only sailing their own life and hardly
can see much of the country
♣♣♣*(8.152)*♣♣♣
Politics are reaction due to business and commerce
♣♣♣*(8.153)*♣♣♣
Right is pure hence no party can own it
♣♣♣*(8.154)*♣♣♣
Leadership is everyday's struggle and fight
♣♣♣*(8.155)*♣♣♣
Ways of politics are worst than war
♣♣♣*(8.156)*♣♣♣
True politician identifies himself with a principle
♣♣♣*(8.157)*♣♣♣
Oratory is fundamental foundation to politics
♣♣♣*(8.158)*♣♣♣
Uncertainty and unpredictability is essence of politics

♣♣♣*(8.159)*♣♣♣
By default people are against everything all the time initially
♣♣♣*(8.160)*♣♣♣
Never play politics with personnel jobs
♣♣♣*(8.161)*♣♣♣
Politicians whatever they commit, even they themselves don't
agree  at times
♣♣♣*(8.162)*♣♣♣
Perception of common interests requires continuous iterations
♣♣♣*(8.163)*♣♣♣
Switching party stand is habit
♣♣♣*(8.164)*♣♣♣
For many, politics are question of business
♣♣♣*(8.165)*♣♣♣
Never use faith as basis of political organization
♣♣♣*(8.166)*♣♣♣
If you want to participate in politics you are likely to lose your
freedom
♣♣♣*(8.167)*♣♣♣
War is a result of continued and continuation of biased
♣♣♣*(8.168)*♣♣♣
Stability and reform are basic elements in politics
♣♣♣*(8.169)*♣♣♣
Politics has no heart but only mind
♣♣♣*(8.170)*♣♣♣
The difference between balance and imbalance of power can
escalate up to war
♣♣♣*(8.171)*♣♣♣
Never losing temper is necessity in political life
♣♣♣*(8.172)*♣♣♣
Misstatements are common
♣♣♣*(8.173)*♣♣♣
In politics one is worst than another
♣♣♣*(8.174)*♣♣♣
Politics needs no preparation

♣♣♣(8.175)♣♣♣
New world needs new type of political system
♣♣♣(8.176)♣♣♣
There is no perception difference between ally and enemy
♣♣♣(8.177)♣♣♣
Unbalanced budget causes indiscipline
♣♣♣(8.178)♣♣♣
People seek help from the government for restoring their lost
confidence
♣♣♣(8.179)♣♣♣
Object of government is happiness of common man
♣♣♣(8.180)♣♣♣
State should be a beneficent one to its citizens
♣♣♣(8.181)♣♣♣
Government objective should never be glory
♣♣♣(8.182)♣♣♣
It is time waste to find logic behind partiality
♣♣♣(8.183)♣♣♣
Governance should be such that it should be easy for anyone to
do good and very difficult to do wrong
♣♣♣(8.184)♣♣♣
No government can certainly manage economic weather
♣♣♣(8.185)♣♣♣
Governance is power in trust
♣♣♣(8.186)♣♣♣
All governments are selfish
♣♣♣(8.187)♣♣♣
Socialism enables quick change of policy rather build it up again
♣♣♣(8.188)♣♣♣
Government should be either way enough to give and enough
to take away
♣♣♣(8.189)♣♣♣
Evils in government exists only in its abuses
♣♣♣(8.190)♣♣♣

The problem for growth is business external environment is fixed by government

♣♣♣(8.191)♣♣♣

Government should do things what an individual cannot do

♣♣♣(8.192)♣♣♣

There is difference between being in office and being in power

♣♣♣(8.193)♣♣♣

Government has to preserve assets

♣♣♣(8.194)♣♣♣

There cannot be good laws without infrastructure to implement

♣♣♣(8.195)♣♣♣

World is governed by little wisdom

♣♣♣(8.196)♣♣♣

It is important to know nation is at service of leaders or leaders are at service of nation

♣♣♣(8.197)♣♣♣

Government protects one from another

♣♣♣(8.198)♣♣♣

Secrecy is essential in some matter of state

♣♣♣(8.199)♣♣♣

Restraints of government are reflection of true individual liberty

♣♣♣(8.200)♣♣♣

Effective governance is ability to reach small

♣♣♣(8.201)♣♣♣

Every citizen has right to expect fair deal from government

♣♣♣(8.202)♣♣♣

Goodness of good act is only reality by acting with good intention

♣♣♣(8.203)♣♣♣

Freedom is not given it is claimed

♣♣♣(8.204)♣♣♣

A man feels free or not at his freedom is his will

♣♣♣(8.205)♣♣♣

Power concentration is not freedom

♣♣♣*(8.206)*♣♣♣

Freedom cannot be right to do wrong

♣♣♣*(8.207)*♣♣♣

Right to be free is first step to freedom

♣♣♣*(8.208)*♣♣♣

Freedom comes from understanding laws not from independence from laws

♣♣♣*(8.209)*♣♣♣

Freedom can be never free

♣♣♣*(8.210)*♣♣♣

Freedom is given for restructuring yourself for good

♣♣♣*(8.211)*♣♣♣

Human yearning for freedom can't be destroyed by anyone

♣♣♣*(8.212)*♣♣♣

Haters of freedom never discuss they just tarnish freedom

♣♣♣*(8.213)*♣♣♣

It is sometimes better not to possess freedom

♣♣♣*(8.214)*♣♣♣

Freedom is not gained easily

♣♣♣*(8.215)*♣♣♣

Freedom enables perfection

♣♣♣*(8.216)*♣♣♣

Realization of freedom is disciplined overcoming of self

♣♣♣*(8.217)*♣♣♣

Cost of freedom cannot be too high

♣♣♣*(8.218)*♣♣♣

Freedom comes with responsibilities

♣♣♣*(8.219)*♣♣♣

Full freedom is only theoretical lives only in the realm of dreams

♣♣♣*(8.220)*♣♣♣

No freedom no dignity

♣♣♣*(8.221)*♣♣♣

Freedom is invisible

♣♣♣ *(8.222)* ♣♣♣

Liberty cannot be just declaration

♣♣♣ *(8.223)* ♣♣♣

Communism exists inherently and can never be defeated

♣♣♣ *(8.224)* ♣♣♣

Intelligent people are mostly socialists

♣♣♣ *(8.225)* ♣♣♣

Only socialism can survive prolonged

♣♣♣ *(8.226)* ♣♣♣

Politics are all about getting support from disadvantaged

♣♣♣ *(8.227)* ♣♣♣

Disagreement with the policies is due to selfishness and lack of patriotism

♣♣♣ *(8.228)* ♣♣♣

One need to identify real aim and declared aim

♣♣♣ *(8.229)* ♣♣♣

If the government does not implement law it invites everyone to become a law unto himself

♣♣♣ *(8.230)* ♣♣♣

Era of big governance is over

♣♣♣ *(8.231)* ♣♣♣

Where the law ends there anarchy begins

♣♣♣ *(8.232)* ♣♣♣

Power tries to detour to destroy the freedom

♣♣♣ *(8.233)* ♣♣♣

Humans are born to repel invasion of their freedom

♣♣♣ *(8.234)* ♣♣♣

Laws exist to preserve freedom

♣♣♣ *(8.235)* ♣♣♣

Freedom depends on being free

♣♣♣ *(8.236)* ♣♣♣

Everyone today indirectly experiences racism

♣♣♣ *(8.237)* ♣♣♣

No one can cure corruption infection caused by politics

♣♣♣ *(8.238)* ♣♣♣

Power affects not power

♣♣♣ *(8.239)* ♣♣♣

There is no need of government in happiest society

♣♣♣ *(8.240)* ♣♣♣

Politics tends to stick to old policies

♣♣♣ *(8.241)* ♣♣♣

Love and politics are twins

♣♣♣ *(8.242)* ♣♣♣

Trust is must for existence of government

♣♣♣ *(8.243)* ♣♣♣

Unlimited freedom without law compliance will make one
unpredictable and uncontrollable

♣♣♣

# 9.LIFE PLANNING AND WORK PLANNING

You may have Wealth, people, skills, resources, education, knowhow but if you don't know how to plan then you will certain to fail in personal and professional life's.

Most people either can't understand Planning or don't know how to plan in either way they fail.

Consistent planning will surely make you to move forward against all odds even if you don't have best talent.

Good Planning can replace and substitute your many lacking's.

Plans and Planning are most crucial part of life and work achievement in this modern and complex world.

Most of the Plans fail due to confusion & non understanding by individuals.

We have presented more than 175 nos Modern TIPS under 39 aspects of Planning for understanding, preparing and implementing Plans & Planning for life and work.

# 9.Life Planning and Work Planning
## *Contents*

♣♣♣*(9.1)*♣♣♣
# TYPES & PLAN
♣♣♣*(9.1.1)*♣♣♣
There is nothing like quick planning or slow planning,  but all plans must be standard plans based on at least 75% inputs.

♣♣♣*(9.2)*♣♣♣
# CHRACTERISTICS & PLAN
♣♣♣*(9.2.1)*♣♣♣
Planning needs to be  consistent
♣♣♣*(9.2.2)*♣♣♣
Plan should be founded on your strengths.
♣♣♣*(9.2.3)*♣♣♣
Planning should be comprehensive and complete.
♣♣♣*(9.2.4)*♣♣♣
Plan is a meant to achieve goals.
♣♣♣*(9.2.5)*♣♣♣
Planning is irreversible.
♣♣♣*(9.2.6)*♣♣♣
Plan should remove confusion.

♣♣♣*(9.3)*♣♣♣
# CONSULTANTS & PLAN
♣♣♣*(9.3.1)*♣♣♣
Hire business consultants and specialists as and when needed.
♣♣♣*(9.3.2)*♣♣♣
Always talk to experts of the field.
♣♣♣*(9.3.3)*♣♣♣
Use consultants for independent & impartial oversight.

♣♣♣*(9.4)*♣♣♣
# CONTINGENCY & PLAN
♣♣♣*(9.4.1)*♣♣♣
Surprises are common, however it is planning that shall makes us to manage anticipated surprises.

♣♣♣*(9.4.2)*♣♣♣
Plan strategies should be sound enough to address exigencies and contingencies.

♣♣♣*(9.5)*♣♣♣
## CONTROL & PLANNING
♣♣♣*(9.5.1)*♣♣♣
Intervention based on retrospective is important
♣♣♣*(9.5.2)*♣♣♣
Planning gives right moment and time to intervene and correct.
♣♣♣*(9.5.3)*♣♣♣
Either you control your time or you let time bury you.
♣♣♣*(9.5.4)*♣♣♣
Time propagates faults & mistakes, hence timely intervention is must.
♣♣♣*(9.5.5)*♣♣♣
Administrative controls are necessary for some activities.

♣♣♣*(9.6)*♣♣♣
## CULTURE & PLANNING
♣♣♣*(9.6.1)*♣♣♣
Create a honesty protected & optimistic environment for expressing freely.
♣♣♣*(9.6.2)*♣♣♣
You cannot achieve your objectives with right people in wrong environment.
♣♣♣*(9.6.3)*♣♣♣
Individuals behaviour is driven by prevailing organization culture.

♣♣♣*(9.7)*♣♣♣
## DIRECTION & PLAN
♣♣♣*(9.7.1)*♣♣♣
Just by repetition you can't change your course and direction or get different results.

♣♣♣*(9.7.2)*♣♣♣
Where we are, is not that important, but where are we heading
is important.
♣♣♣*(9.7.3)*♣♣♣
Speedy execution is important to avoid and prevent changes in
direction.
♣♣♣*(9.7.4)*♣♣♣
You will automatically find road as long as you are hooked to
your objective.
♣♣♣*(9.7.5)*♣♣♣
Without aim you are lost individual.
♣♣♣*(9.7.6)*♣♣♣
Unfocused objectives  time duration is your misdirection and
off track.

♣♣♣*(9.8)*♣♣♣
# ECONOMY & PLAN
♣♣♣*(9.8.1)*♣♣♣
Commercial existence has to be a reality for survival.
♣♣♣*(9.8.2)*♣♣♣
There are costs you can a)avoid, b)reduce , c)postpone,
d)control
♣♣♣*(9.8.3)*♣♣♣
Project gestation period has direct impact on project viability.

♣♣♣*(9.9)*♣♣♣
# ERRORS & PLAN
♣♣♣*(9.9.1)*♣♣♣
Planning prevents errors and blunders.
♣♣♣*(9.9.2)*♣♣♣
Even best people do make mistakes.
♣♣♣*(9.9.3)*♣♣♣
Most of the error situations are predictable and controllable.

♣♣♣*(9.10)*♣♣♣

# FAILURE & PLAN

♣♣♣*(9.10.1)*♣♣♣

Stopped trying is biggest failure.


♣♣♣*(9.11)*♣♣♣

# FEEDBACK  & PLAN

♣♣♣*(9.11.1)*♣♣♣

There can't be repeated same feedback status again and again when internal as well as external circumstances keep changing.

♣♣♣*(9.11.2)*♣♣♣

9Executed plan gives experiences to carry forward to next projects.

♣♣♣*(9.11.3)*♣♣♣

You need to learn from past experiences and plan future but you can't plan future on past.

♣♣♣*(9.11.4)*♣♣♣

Get regular feedback both routines and happenings.


♣♣♣*(9.12)*♣♣♣

# HUMAN RESOURCES & PLANNING

♣♣♣*(9.12.1)*♣♣♣

At crucial times there may be possible brain drain. Talented people are expected to leave. Never allow monopoly in work, make everyone capable by encouraging sharing of knowledge.

♣♣♣*(9.12.2)*♣♣♣

Delegating is uncommon skill, you need to educate others.

♣♣♣*(9.12.3)*♣♣♣

All great works had great teams.

♣♣♣*(9.12.4)*♣♣♣

A true professional constantly seeks purpose.

♣♣♣*(9.12.5)*♣♣♣

All successful living people are committed to dedicated goals.

♣♣♣*(9.12.6)*♣♣♣

Successful people are exceptional people in whatever they do.

♣♠♣*(9.13)*♣♠♣

# IMAGINATION  & PLANNING

♣♠♣*(9.13.1)*♣♠♣

Memory nourishes imagination.

♣♠♣*(9.13.2)*♣♠♣

You can't create anything constructive without imagination.

♣♠♣*(9.13.3)*♣♠♣

Your imagination creates smoke screen for your reality.

♣♠♣*(9.13.4)*♣♠♣

Imagination is the eye of heart.

♣♠♣*(9.13.5)*♣♠♣

Imagination is a seed to change.

♣♠♣*(9.13.6)*♣♠♣

Our lives are more burdened by imagination and fiction than realities.

♣♠♣*(9.13.7)*♣♠♣

Imagination is men's unnatural ability bestowed by God.

♣♠♣*(9.13.8)*♣♠♣

Imagination counters reality.

♣♠♣*(9.13.9)*♣♠♣

Humans cannot distinguish difference between imagination and reality.

♣♠♣*(9.13.10)*♣♠♣

When imagination is lost oversight is lost.

♣♠♣*(9.14)*♣♠♣

# IMPLEMENTATION CHRACTERISTICS & PLAN

♣♠♣*(9.14.1)*♣♠♣

Sudden gains are not expected by planning

♣♠♣*(9.14.2)*♣♠♣

Execution needs to be consistent.

♣♠♣*(9.15)*♣♠♣

## IMPLEMENTATION & PLAN

♣♠♣*(9.15.1)*♣♠♣

Good plan helps in making us to execute at our best.

♣♣♣(9.15.2)♣♣♣

Every big objective achievement is a result of thousands of forward small steps.

♣♣♣(9.15.3)♣♣♣

tomorrow.

♣♣♣(9.15.4)♣♣♣

Just focus on scheduled current objective.

♣♣♣(9.15.5)♣♣♣

Decision shall be converted into reality by interested parties at the earliest.

♣♣♣(9.15.6)♣♣♣

All decisions and activities execution must be not on past status but on current status.

♣♣♣(9.15.7)♣♣♣

Preparation for doing consumes time, energy and resources.

♣♣♣(9.15.8)♣♣♣

What goal do you wish to achieve? Is it short term, medium term and long term goal?

♣♣♣(9.15.9)♣♣♣

Plan triggers sequential and consequential activities in execution.

♣♣♣(9.15.10)♣♣♣

How much time do you need preparing for planning activities? There your real experience is called for.

♣♣♣(9.15.11)♣♣♣

It is very difficult  to live to the purpose.

♣♣♣(9.16)♣♣♣

# ITERATION & PLAN

♣♣♣(9.16.1)♣♣♣

You need to improve your plans on both positive or negative happenings.

♣♣♣(9.16.2)♣♣♣

Everyone and everything changes with time, hence you need to re-plan.

*♣♣♣(9.16.3)♣♣♣*

We learn from mistakes to make smarter plans for the future by iteration.

*♣♣♣(9.16.4)♣♣♣*

All assumptions needs to be checked for their validity time to time and changed if necessary.

*♣♣♣(9.17)♣♣♣*
## LEARNING & PLAN

*♣♣♣(9.17.1)♣♣♣*

Task needs Continuous and continual learning to the requirement of execution and changing circumstances. Learning is part of plan. You can never find perfect person, you have to develop perfect person.

*♣♣♣(9.17.2)♣♣♣*

Share learning and improvements across organizations.

*♣♣♣(9.17.3)♣♣♣*

You should learn from time.

*♣♣♣(9.17.4)♣♣♣*

Learning critical attributes for success.

*♣♣♣(9.18)♣♣♣*
## MICRO & MACRO & PLANS

*♣♣♣(9.18.1)♣♣♣*

A plan provides insight as well as oversight depending on level.

*♣♣♣(9.18.2)♣♣♣*

Plan gives you a beautiful oversight by connecting disconnected or isolated activities.

*♣♣♣(9.19)♣♣♣*
## MONITORING & PLAN

*♣♣♣(9.19.1)♣♣♣*

You can't focus simultaneously on too many things, there are human biological limitations.

*♣♣(9.19.2)♣♣*

Success has no shortcuts only one highway however failure has too many ways hence one need to be vigilant and attentive.

*♣♣(9.19.3)♣♣*

Trend internal environment and external environment for noticing occurring changes.

*♣♣(9.19.4)♣♣*

Continuously monitor what is most important to main objectives.

*♣♣(9.19.5)♣♣*

Use performance indicators that reflect implementation status and trend indicators. Performance indicators enables to early detection of undesirable trends.

*♣♣(9.20)♣♣*

# OBJECTIVES & PLAN

*♣♣(9.20.1)♣♣*

Effective plan shares common objectives as a individual objectives at every milestone.

*♣♣(9.20.2)♣♣*

Objectives shall be respected as well as treated seriously.

*♣♣(9.20.3)♣♣*

You have to fix common values for your team w.r.t objectives.

*♣♣(9.20.4)♣♣*

A plan enables to see projected nearest path.

*♣♣(9.20.5)♣♣*

When same objective is individually visualizes as well as collectively visualized it is a shared purpose with oneness.

*♣♣(9.20.6)♣♣*

One can individually contribute to purpose only with shared vision.

*♣♣(9.20.7)♣♣*

Your success is your tenacity to your aim.

♣♣♣*(9.20.8)*♣♣♣

What you do and How you do it that contributes to your objectives.


♣♣♣*(9.21)*♣♣♣
# PLANNING & PLAN
♣♣♣*(9.21.1)*♣♣♣

Plans without planning is worthless,  they never contribute constructively and makes situation even worse as well as irreversible.


♣♣♣*(9.22)*♣♣♣
# PREREQUISITES & PLAN
♣♣♣*(9.22.1)*♣♣♣

Understand, understand, understand before planning

♣♣♣*(9.22.2)*♣♣♣

Effective plan is based on at least more than 75% inputs required.

♣♣♣*(9.22.3)*♣♣♣

First a plan needs thorough understanding of all aspects of your objectives or goals that you would like to achieve.

♣♣♣*(9.22.4)*♣♣♣

There is an entry threshold in order consider an activity to be part of a plan based on its importance.

♣♣♣*(9.22.5)*♣♣♣

Success seeks preparation.


♣♣♣*(9.23)*♣♣♣
# PRIORITY  & PLAN
♣♣♣*(9.23.1)*♣♣♣

Plan gives clarity to distinguish between what is important and what is unimportant as well as what is urgent and what is not urgent.

♣♣♣*(9.23.2)*♣♣♣

It essential to ignore unimportant activities.

♣♣♣*(9.23.3)*♣♣♣

Key to successful planning being able to focus on what is important.

♣♣♣*(9.23.4)*♣♣♣

Time is limited hence you have to prioritize tasks at hand based on their importance as well as urgency w.r.t. objectives.

♣♣♣*(9.24)*♣♣♣

## PROBLEMS & PLANNING

♣♣♣*(9.24.1)*♣♣♣

You have to breath the problem fully with all requisites.

♣♣♣*(9.24.2)*♣♣♣

Facilitate meetings to solve the problems and bottlenecks.

♣♣♣*(9.24.3)*♣♣♣

Plan enables timely and early detect initiation of a problem much before it aggravates into a irreversible big problem in a long duration.

♣♣♣*(9.24.4)*♣♣♣

Foreseen hurdle or bottleneck is half problem solved.

♣♣♣*(9.24.5)*♣♣♣

Unexpected hurdles are avoided as long as you stick to your objectives.

♣♣♣*(9.24.6)*♣♣♣

Creativity and experience comes to rescue for addressing bottlenecks and delays.

♣♣♣*(9.24.7)*♣♣♣

Whenever you encounter a problem prepare a problem statement defining problem in all perspectives for finding possible solutions.

♣♣♣*(9.24.8)*♣♣♣

Brainstorming is good idea for breaking ice while dealing with bottlenecks in planning.

♣♣♣*(9.25)*♣♣♣

## PRODUCTIVITY  & PLAN

♣♣♣*(9.25.1)*♣♣♣

Perfect plan creates synergy of shared interests.

♣♣♣*(9.26)*♣♣♣

# REGULATION & PLAN

♣♣♣*(9.26.1)*♣♣♣

All plans have rules.

♣♣♣*(9.26.2)*♣♣♣

All legal, statutory and regulatory compliance,  permits, licenses and permissions activities must be planned much ahead. They are the responsibility of strategists.

♣♣♣*(9.27)*♣♣♣

# PROGRESS & PLAN

♣♣♣*(9.27.1)*♣♣♣

You have to overcome past for marching into future.

♣♣♣*(9.27.2)*♣♣♣

Forward growth is a symptom of healthiness.

♣♣♣*(9.28)*♣♣♣

# RESOURCES & PLANNING

♣♣♣*(9.28.1)*♣♣♣

Adequate support is the basic requisite for a plan to convert a dream into a reality.

♣♣♣*(9.28.2)*♣♣♣

No activity can be integral part of plan unless it is backed by required resources. Otherwise it is a clear violation of essence of a plan.

♣♣♣*(9.28.3)*♣♣♣

Good plan enables to exploit synergy in resources utilization.

♣♣♣*(9.28.4)*♣♣♣

Without vision all resources values are lost.

♣♣♣*(9.28.5)*♣♣♣

One can deploy minimum resources at strong milestones and maximum resources at weak milestones and activities in a plan.

♣♣♣*(9.29)*♣♣♣

# RESPONSIBILITIES & PLANNING

♣♣♣*(9.29.1)*♣♣♣

Who and when are most important part of task.

♣♣♣*(9.29.2)*♣♣♣

Never delegate unique tasks what you can alone do better.

♣♣♣*(9.29.3)*♣♣♣

If you are honest to your objectives you automatically seek accountability from your reporting.

♣♣♣*(9.29.4)*♣♣♣

For each activity someone should  dream it and own its time.

♣♣♣*(9.30)*♣♣♣

# REVIEW & PLANNING

♣♣♣*(9.30.1)*♣♣♣

You can maintain momentum of execution only be periodic as well as non periodic reviews.

♣♣♣*(9.30.2)*♣♣♣

In light of emergence of new kind of unknown information review w.r.t.  their possible influence on your plan objectives.

♣♣♣*(9.30.3)*♣♣♣

Always talk in terms of objectives not in terms of specific person in reviews.

♣♣♣*(9.30.4)*♣♣♣

You can't cover everything in review, you have to have some strategic control points depending upon level of your review w.r t. Objectives.

♣♣♣*(9.30.5)*♣♣♣

Do your short-term, medium term and long-term goals are they consist and aligned with your objectives.

♣♣♣*(9.30.6)*♣♣♣

Independent verification review of all important activities is essential.

♣♣♣*(9.30.7)*♣♣♣

A healthy questioning attitude can overcome individual temptations and can divert all towards focusing on objectives.

♣♣♣ *(9.31)* ♣♣♣
## RISK & PLAN
♣♣♣ *(9.31.1)* ♣♣♣
There is associated less gains and high inherent risks in adopting shortcuts bypassing main plans.

♣♣♣ *(9.31.2)* ♣♣♣
Periodically review business risks being faced in short-term, medium term and in long-term.

♣♣♣ *(9.31.3)* ♣♣♣
Risk is integral to a plan. No risk plan is a riskiest plan.

♣♣♣ *(9.31.4)* ♣♣♣
Most dangerous risk is being not honest with ourselves by self reflection.

♣♣♣ *(9.31.5)* ♣♣♣
Plan should conquer all risks.

♣♣♣ *(9.32)* ♣♣♣
## SKILLS & PLANNING
♣♣♣ *(9.32.1)* ♣♣♣
Beyond certain level you need skills to manage and coordinate.

♣♣♣ *(9.32.2)* ♣♣♣
Better management is feasible with your strengths.

♣♣♣ *(9.32.3)* ♣♣♣
Managing is managing for better results.

♣♣♣ *(9.32.4)* ♣♣♣
Even god will help a man who fights with his strengths.

♣♣♣ *(9.32.5)* ♣♣♣
Opportunities find people with creativity and skills.

♣♣♣ *(9.33)* ♣♣♣
## STRATEGISTS & PLANNING
♣♣♣ *(9.33.1)* ♣♣♣

Strategists are visionaries only they understand realities.

♣♣♣(9.33.2)♣♣♣

A plan answers majority of questions of execution, except few unanswered questions, that must be and solved by strategists.

♣♣♣(9.33.3)♣♣♣

It is the responsibility of strategists to mobilize resources for planned activities with their oversight.

♣♣♣(9.34)♣♣♣

## SUCCESS & PLAN

♣♣♣(9.34.1)♣♣♣

Best plans makes definite big difference though they never achieved intended objectives.

♣♣♣(19.34.2)♣♣♣

Cooperation, shared vision and collective work is synergy to productivity and achievement.

♣♣♣(9.34.3)♣♣♣

Time reveals actual status the truth.

♣♣♣(9.34.4)♣♣♣

End of a plan need not necessarily be good.

♣♣♣(9.34.5)♣♣♣

Success requires unconditional acceptance of its challenges on its way.

♣♣♣(9.34.6)♣♣♣

Discipline, hard work and commonsense are requisites for success.

♣♣♣(9.34.7)♣♣♣

At the end of the day only success only counted.

♣♣♣(9.34.8)♣♣♣

Success creates a brand image.

♣♣♣(9.34.9)♣♣♣

Achieving success will compensate for pain of all repeated failures.

♣♣♣(9.34.10)♣♣♣

Success automatically labels you as good.

*♣♣♣(9.34.11)♣♣♣*

Successful people always have an attitude to question as well as seeking accountability.

*♣♣♣(9.34.12)♣♣♣*

Right or wrong are labeled only after achieving success .

*♣♣♣(9.34.13)♣♣♣*

Aroma of success is sweet.

*♣♣♣(9.34.14)♣♣♣*

You plan either to succeed or to fail, there is no third option.

*♣♣♣(9.34.15)♣♣♣*

People never try to color accomplishments.

*♣♣♣(9.35)♣♣♣*

## TEAMS & PLAN

*♣♣♣(9.35.1)♣♣♣*

Despite differences you need to keep people aligned and working collectively together.

*♣♣♣(9.35.2)♣♣♣*

Not just with plans but you need to empower your teams with all necessary inputs and resources required.

*♣♣♣(9.36)♣♣♣*

## TIME & PLAN

*♣♣♣(9.36.1)♣♣♣*

Time is a plan.

*♣♣♣(9.36.2)♣♣♣*

Un-respected time can robs you.

*♣♣♣(9.36.3)♣♣♣*

Time reveals.

*♣♣♣(9.36.4)♣♣♣*

Time can't accommodate everything.

*♣♣♣(9.36.5)♣♣♣*

Time gives end to everything.

*♣♣♣(9.36.6)♣♣♣*

Timing is the most important component.

**(9.36.7)**
Time says nothing but time passed says many things.

**(9.36.8)**
Time we wasted is more crucial than time left.

**(9.36.9)**
Past time and present times are interwoven hence present time is most important time.

**(9.36.10)**
There is no salvage for time waste.

**(9.36.11)**
Time is a productivity tool.

**(9.36.12)**
Be faithful to time.

**(9.36.13)**
Burden of time increases exponentially proportional to wasted time.

**(9.36.14)**
9One feels easy or difficult activities depending on available time.

**(9.36.15)**
Doing time is more important than talking time.

**(9.36.16)**
Perfectionism need not be required for all activities probably optimism may be adequate. Perfectionism is consumes infinite time.

**(9.36.17)**
You have to achieve measured progress in a specified time.


**(9.37)**
## TOOLS  & PLAN
**(9.37.1)**
Use business productivity tools.


**(9.38)**
## TRUST & PLANNING

♣♣♣ *(9.38.1)* ♣♣♣

All decisions must based on understanding and trust by competent personnel.

♣♣♣ *(9.38.2)* ♣♣♣

We can't monitor and check everything every time. Hence trust, loyalty and integrity are essentials and must.

♣♣♣ *(9.39)* ♣♣♣

# PLAN & BAD

♣♣♣ *(9.39.1)* ♣♣♣

A bad plan is non flexible to change or alter. It makes things irreversible.

♣♣♣

# Acknowledgements

I am thankful to my daughter Gummadi Pavani, mother Baby Samrajyam Gummadi and wife Swapna Gummadi with who's cooperation and help I could author this book.

**VIJAYKUMAR GUMMADI**

# About Author

Mr VIJAYKUMAR GUMMADI is a Chemical Engineering & Business Management(MBA) Professional and a Nuclear Technology Specialist and Certified International Project Management Expert with more than thirty five years of experience in eight industries of Six States.

Developing Creative, innovative Business & Management Skills and Techniques and writing books are his Area of Self Interest.

He has Authored many books that includes Best Selling International Paperbacks  and e-Books.

For other Book details please visit last pages of this book.

## UNLEASHING CREATIVITY, 2133 QUOTES THAT WILL MAKE YOU RETHIK

2133 nos creative unique quotes covering all areas i.e. life, love, work, success, business, motivation, spirutuality etc . Most up-to-date thinking book in the world. Extraordinary book to rise above day to day thinking.

ISBN 9781684946129 (ENGLISH)
ISBN 9798890021366 (TELUGU)

## POSITIVE QUOTATIONS & TIPS

Beautiful compilation of life and work affirming 1000 nos positive quotes & tips from greatest thinking minds covering love, feminism, money, happiness, human nature, anxiety, depression, Diet, obesity, politics, governance, life, Work.

ISBN 9798888057704 (ENGLISH)
ISBN 9798890666321 (TELUGU)

## POSITIVE TIPS FOR STRESS

Stress is part of modern lifestyle. We can't do anything other than managing stress in modern life.This Book presents 501 nos life changing tips for managing and coping with stress.

ISBN 9798889519638 (ENGLISH)
ISBN 9798889592914 (TELUGU)

## EASY MANAGING GUIDE FOR MODERN MANAGERS & EMPLOYEES

This book brings out 825 nos easy & immensely practical tips and sound advise under 75 managing aspects of organisation for helping modern managers and employees.

ISBN 9798885464321 (ENGLISH)
ISBN 9798889233923 (TELUGU)

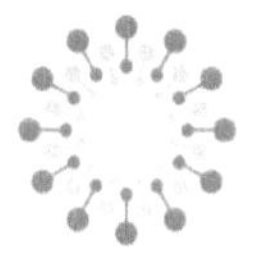


## GOOD OFFICE TIPS

This book presents 710 nos useful tips for managing modern offices and organisations for implementing wonderful practices for improvement. These tips are based on modern time tested wisdom.

ISBN 9798890028129 (ENGLISH)
ISBN 9798890674487 (TELUGU)

**Available at AMAZON and FLIPKART**